Praise for *Seeking Wisdom* and *The Listening Path*

"Julia Cameron's new book, *Seeking Wisdom,* carries on the author's tradition of magically changing lives, hearts, habits, and attitudes. Julia writes about her own life and about writing and living, and in this six-week guide to contemplation, prayer, and seeking the living presence, Julia does again what she has done since writing *The Artist's Way*: she leads us into the real questions and answers that lie in our path, points to contemplation of the Higher Power in our creative inner lives, and points us to the spiritual approach—prayer, work, writing, and living. She is a master of her craft of giving to others what her inner guides have taught her, and I promise you will come away from reading her new book, as I did, with renewed creative zest and energy, as well as insight into your own spiritual possibilities as a creative person. Get this book—*Seeking Wisdom*; it holds magical wisdom and genuine truth."
—Judy Collins, singer, songwriter, author

"In *Seeking Wisdom,* the prolific Julia Cameron continues her work as a masterful guide, offering a path of creative recovery by asking us to personalize our sense of God through our own intimate practice of prayer. Both grounded and innovative, this book casts writing as praying on the page to everything larger than us. Bring your whole self to the journey of this book and you will touch the eternal link between creativity and spirituality. This book will help you come alive. It will help you play your instrument and sing your song."
—Mark Nepo, author of *The Book of Soul* and *Finding Inner Courage*

"Julia Cameron brought a new approach to creativity to the world with her extraordinary book *The Artist's Way*. Now, in *The Listening Path*, she takes us into a completely different dimension of creativity: the ability to listen at deeper and deeper levels. As a lifelong student of the art of listening, I can tell you there is nothing quite like this book. I encourage you to read *The Listening Path* and make use of its life-changing gifts."

—Gay Hendricks, PhD, *New York Times* bestselling author of *The Big Leap* and *Conscious Luck*

"Julia Cameron has done it again. In *The Listening Path*, she gently guides us to become more in tune with ourselves, our world, each other, and beyond—bringing more clarity, connection, and joy into our lives. Whether you're a seasoned creator or just getting started, *The Listening Path* will guide you to access the treasure trove of wisdom that lives within, and in the world around you."

—Amber Rae, author of *Choose Wonder Over Worry*

WRITE FOR LIFE

WRITE FOR LIFE

Creative Tools for
Every Writer

A SIX-WEEK ARTIST'S WAY PROGRAM

JULIA CAMERON

ST. MARTIN'S
ESSENTIALS
NEW YORK

First published in the United States by St. Martin's Essentials, an imprint of St. Martin's Publishing Group

WRITE FOR LIFE. Copyright © 2022 by Julia Cameron. All rights reserved. Printed in Canada. For information, address St. Martin's Publishing Group, 120 Broadway, New York, NY 10271.

www.stmartins.com

The Library of Congress Cataloging-in-Publication Data is available upon request.

ISBN 978-1-250-86627-1 (trade paperback)
ISBN 978-1-250-86628-8 (ebook)

Our books may be purchased in bulk for promotional, educational, or business use. Please contact your local bookseller or the Macmillan Corporate and Premium Sales Department at 1-800-221-7945, extension 5442, or by email at MacmillanSpecialMarkets@macmillan.com.

First Edition: 2023

10 9 8 7 6 5 4 3 2

To Julianna McCarthy, for her poetry, prayers,
and passion

ACKNOWLEDGMENTS

**Joel Fotinos, muse and fuselighter, for his steady,
grace-filled inspiration**

Dr. Jeannette Aycock, for her persistent positivity
Jennifer Bassey, for her inspired faith
Tyler Beattie, for his enthusiasm and creativity
Domenica Frenzel, for her passion and prayers
Natalie Goldberg, for her powerful example
Gerard Hackett, for his thoughtful input
Gwen Hawkes, for her meticulous care
Nick Kapustinsky, for his intelligence and insight
Rena Keane, for her generous faith
Laura Leddy, for her graceful support
Emma Lively, for her inspiration and integrity
Jacob Nordby, for his prayers and prose
Scottie Pierce, for her daily practice
Susan Raihofer, for her discernment and daring
Ed Towle, for his humor and acuity

CONTENTS

HOW TO USE THIS BOOK

Write for Life is a six-week program for anyone working on a writing project, from the first-time writer to the seasoned one. This book is an invitation to begin, stick with, and finish your project. Consider it a companion on your journey from conception to completion. These pages compile the tips and tricks I myself have relied on to write more than forty books—including this one. It is my hope that this book will serve you as both a guide over the next six weeks, and a handbook to be returned to as you continue writing, well beyond the next six weeks. This book will get you in motion, keep you in motion, and serve as a reference as you finish your draft and move into the revision phase.

It is the act of writing that makes us writers. If you have a desire to write, that desire is worth listening to—and acting upon. I have been a full-time writer for more than fifty years, writing books, poetry, music, plays, movies, and novels. This is my love letter to writing, and to writers, sharing the tools I have used—and that anyone can use—to write for life.

WEEK ONE

PRIMING THE PUMP

There are several basic tools that serve as a bedrock for productive writing. With these tools in place, it is possible to set the stage for longevity as a writer. This week, you will prime the pump—readying yourself for the long-term commitment between writer and writing project. By committing to these tools and examining your approach to your writing, you will set in motion a healthy, sustainable process that will carry you through the next six weeks—and beyond.

INTRODUCTION

I love to write. I'm seventy-three years old, and I have been writing full-time since I was eighteen. That's fifty-five years—a long-running romance.

I *love* to write. Pen to the page, I find clarity and order.

I love to write, and so I do it daily. Right now I am sitting in my library, in my big leather writing chair, and I am, yes, writing. My little dog Lily, a Westie, sprawls at my feet. "Good dog, Lily," I croon. But Lily is not a good dog. She is a very naughty dog, and chief among her misdeeds is a fondness for pens. Lily is a writer's dog, I joke. I settle in to write and Lily settles in to steal my pen. I move my hand across the page, and whenever I stop, Lily pounces. She grabs my pen and scampers off, only to emerge minutes later with a disemboweled pen and a jaunty black mustache.

"Lily, I'm trying to write," I scold her, but the game

of "get the pen" gives her great pleasure. She jumps on my lap, landing squarely on my notebook. She grabs my pen and scampers away. So now I am writing with pen number two. What I want to write about is writing itself.

I'll start with a flora and fauna report: my roses are blooming, scarlet and white. Songbirds carol from the junipers. Underfoot, quick-witted gray lizards scoot clear of the path. Lily darts in pursuit. It is only early May, but Santa Fe is enjoying an early summer. Today's day is hot and hazy. The mountains are blurred. Walking with Lily, I am quickly thirsty. When cars pass us on our dirt road, clouds of dust linger in the air. I pause and wait for the dust to settle before pressing on. Our walks are a daily discipline I set for myself. On the days when our walks are aborted—too much wind or rain—Lily grows restless, pacing the Saltillo tiles of my adobe house. "Lily," I tell her, "we'll go tomorrow."

When nightfall comes, Lily settles down. Last night's three-quarter moon cleared the mountains as a silvery disc. Tonight the moon will be near full and its glow will grace the garden, an inviting light to write by, and so I write.

Writing, like walking, is a daily discipline. Like Lily, I grow restless if the routine is skipped. And so now I take pen to page, writing the details of my day, knowing that writing leads to writing. For six months now, I have been between books. Officially not writing, except for my Morning Pages. I have found myself writing cards and letters to my far-flung friends. Inspired by my example, many of them have written me back, our cards crossing in the mail.

"We live so far apart," my friend Jennifer had taken to moaning. I carefully selected the cards I sent to her—photographic images of New Mexico winging their way to Florida. I sent a picture of our cathedral, of a ristra—a string of red chili peppers, of a cactus flower in bloom.

Jennifer would be delighted by the photos and my terse, card-sized notes. She no longer complains of our separation. The written word and pictures soothe her psyche as no amount of telephone chat can.

Sitting at my dining room table, I write out my notecards. I am provoked to write with great specificity. A card with roses to Laura finds me reporting on my own roses. A card with an owl, and I am telling my mentor, poet Julianna McCarthy, how very much I appreciate her wisdom. My daughter, Domenica, a horse lover, received a card of ponies and a note inquiring her progress with the young horse she is schooling. Each note tells the recipient they are cherished. I have taken the time to write. Out at a cafe, I enjoy a soy chai latte. I write to my colleague Emma Lively, knowing her preference for a fancy cappuccino.

"I got your card," Laura reports a quick three days later. Her card features rambling roses—tall like Laura herself. "It was beautiful," she continues. Seated again at my dining room table, I send her a card of delphiniums. I remember that she likes blue.

"You are beloved," our cards say, and seeing is believing. We hoard our handwritten notes. My daughter reports her cards are strung on yarn, gracing her bookshelf. "They're so happy," she says.

And writing is happy. A potent mood changer, writing tutors us in joy. Putting pen to page, we cherish our lives. We matter, our writing declares. Taking the time and effort to describe our moods, we find those moods lightening. Paying attention, we soothe the anxious part of ourselves that wonders, "What about me?" No longer orphans, we are beloved, and writing to our friend tells them they are beloved. Writing "rights" things between us. The distances common to modern life are diminished. We close the gap of good intentions.

I *love* to write. Writing is powerful. It is an act of

Writing is the only thing that when I do it, I don't feel I should be doing something else.

—GLORIA STEINEM

bravery. As we write, we tell ourselves the truth about how we are—and how we feel. We give the universe our coordinates: "I am precisely here." We give the universe permission to act on our behalf. When we write, we experience synchronicity. Our "luck" improves. Writing is a spiritual path. With each word, we take another step forward. Writing has wisdom in it. It takes courage to see ourselves and our world more clearly. Writing is a commitment to honesty. On the page, in black and white, we see the variables we are dealing with. Writing is a lifeline. I *love* to write.

TOOLS IN PLACE: MORNING PAGES AND ARTIST DATES

As a writer, I credit my daily practice of Morning Pages with giving me the willingness to start where I am. What precisely are Morning Pages? They are three daily pages of longhand morning writing that is strictly stream of consciousness.

The pages clear my head and prioritize my day. I think of them as a potent form of meditation. There is no wrong way to do the pages. You simply keep your hand moving across the page, writing down anything and everything that occurs to you. It is as though you are sending the universe a telegram: "This is what I like, this is what I don't like"—implicit in this, "Please help me." If the pages are meditation, they are also a potent form of prayer.

When I began writing Morning Pages, I needed prayer. I had washed up in the tiny mountain town of Taos, New Mexico, having gone there to sort out my brilliant career. I had written a movie for Jon Voight, and its reception had gone from "brilliant" to radio silence. Discouraged, I had rented a little adobe house at the end of a little dirt road. It was lonely there, and I took up the practice of Morning

Pages to keep myself company. Every day, before my daughter woke up, I would rise and go to the long pine table that faced a large window that held a view of Taos Mountain. Faithfully, I would record the mountain's mood: foggy . . . clear . . . scattered clouds near the summit . . .

"What should I do about my movie?" I would daily ask the pages.

The answer would come back, "Do nothing about your movie. Just write."

And so I would write, about nothing in particular, just daily meanderings. Three daily pages gave me a sense of purpose. It was a manageable amount. The first page and a half were easy. The second page and a half, harder, contained pay dirt: hunches, intuition, insights. The pages were habit forming. They coaxed, cajoled, and tempted me into self-revelation. I became intimate with myself. The pages were a dare; a place where I risked being my authentic self. I wrote—and I loved writing.

One morning, after I finished my pages, I was startled to have a character stroll into view. The character was a woman named Johnny, a plein-air painter who executed a magnificent painting at the end of my pen. Johnny wasn't a movie character. She was—and this startled me—the lead character for a novel. The opening scene rushed through my hand. My mind played catch-up. "You don't have to write movies, you can write books." The onslaught of freedom was heady. I was no longer trapped as a screenwriter. I was liberated, set free. I owed my freedom to the Morning Pages. They had opened an unsuspected inner door. I was grateful to them, and so I kept my daily practice of pages intact, writing my three pages before turning my hand to Johnny and her adventures.

I wrote from summer into fall. Johnny painted the changing foliage. When winter came, she set down her paintbrush. She had fallen in love. Happy, she began painting still lifes: a basket of apples, a pair of pears. If Johnny was happy, her newly found lover served as a muse. I myself was lonely. No lover hovered close at hand. I found myself missing my New York life, chock-full of people and opportunities. One gray morning when the mountain was blocked from view, I wrote "The End." Later that same day, I packed my car for the long drive back to Greenwich Village.

Back in New York after the long drive cross-country, I settled my daughter, Domenica, back into school and I began a practice of long, solo walks, praying for inspiration as to what to write next. A movie? A book? I kept up my practice of Morning Pages, hoping for a clue. Without realizing it, I was establishing a lifelong pattern: first, Morning Pages. Next, a prayerful walk. The cobblestone streets of the West Village became familiar to me. So did the human scale of brownstone houses, shops, and cafes. Then, one afternoon as I walked, I heard a clear directive: "Teach. You must teach."

I had my marching orders, "teach," and I couldn't wriggle out of them. I asked the heavens, "Please, teach what? And where?" My walks expanded and so did my thinking. I would teach what I called "creative unblocking." I would assign my students my own regime—Morning Pages and walks. I would assign them exploratory adventures, like my visit to a bird store, where I befriended an African gray parrot. "Artist Dates," I dubbed these festive, solo expeditions. They filled the well. Taken alone, without dogs or phones or friends, Artist Dates were an exercise in play. It took courage to venture out into the world, on a mission of "just doing something fun." I encouraged my students to go outside of their comfort zone—trying their hand at festive outings that were new to them. "What would entice your inner eight-year-old?" I would ask. "Try that."

All I need is a sheet of paper and something to write with, and then I can turn the world upside down.

—FRIEDRICH NIETZSCHE

I was offered a slot to teach at the New York Feminist Art Institute, which I had never heard of. My first class was to convene on Thursday. Nervous, I found myself excited to share. We met on Spring Street, in a large, airy room with tall windows.

My students were eager learners. Taking to Morning Pages, Artist Dates, and walks, they reported breakthroughs. Janet, a flame-haired blocked director, began directing again. Susan, a blocked writer, began a novel. For everyone, the pages directed the next step. Small steps led to larger ones. The risk of writing daily pages became the risk of making daily art. I found myself thrilled and gratified by my students' achievements. To my surprise, I liked teaching. I liked it very much. My classroom became my laboratory.

A class at a time, I would introduce my students to healing techniques. I would teach and I would learn. Teaching unblocking, I would myself enjoy the freedom of being unblocked. It wasn't a case of teaching instead of writing—it was a case of teaching *releasing* writing. I wrote class notes, which in time evolved into the essays of *The Artist's Way*.

Keeping myself to my practice, I found myself continuing to have breakthroughs. I wrote a new movie at the pages' urging. They pointed out I wasn't trapped in my new identity as a novelist—or a teacher. No, the pages insisted I was simply a writer, and writers simply wrote. I have followed this advice ever since, writing in multiple genres as the pages urged me. I wrote plays, movies, poems, songs—even a crime novel. I wrote them all for the sheer love of writing.

I am often asked if I still do Morning Pages, four decades later. The answer is yes. Upon awakening, I tread to the kitchen, open the refrigerator, and take out last night's coffee pot, filled with this morning's icy brew. Next, I retreat to a living room couch. "Here I am," I write. I set pen to page and record my morning's mood. Nothing is too petty to be described. I write for three pages, jotting down the details of my life. Detail by detail, I record my life. Detail by detail, I am urged to action. Unlike conventional meditation, which lulls the practitioner into calm, Morning Pages spark the practitioner into action. Pages bring up risks: some small, some large. The first time they broach a risk, we may think, "I can't do that." The next time, we may say, "I don't think I can do that." But when the pages persist, we hear ourselves say, "Oh, alright, I'll try it." And, trying it, we find the risk was doable. We have dared to expand. Over time, we learn to resist our own resistance. We cooperate when risks are suggested. Pages tutor us in courage. They change the trajectory of our lives to one of daring. My pages are a telegram to the universe. I know from years of morning writing that these telegrams do not go unanswered. Since I began the practice of Morning Pages, I have published more than forty books.

WALKING TO CREATIVE HEALTH

The day is blue and white: blue skies, white fluffy clouds. The mountain's flank is folded like purple velvet. My little dog is eager for a walk. She sets out on her expedition, trotting briskly. I hurry to keep up. Today is a good day for writing: my walk will prime the pump. Putting one foot in front of the other, a step at a time, I will pray for guidance. I will ask for the inspiration to write what needs to be written. I will hear a hunch, and I will follow where it leads.

In 1938, Brenda Ueland published a book, *If You Want to Write*. It details the care and maintenance of the writer as a creative artist. It is shrewd, personal, and pragmatic. She advocates walking, believing, as I do, that inspiration comes to a body in motion. She wrote, "Think of yourself

as an incandescent power illuminated and perhaps forever talked to by God and his messengers. Since you are
like no other being ever created since the beginning of
time, you are incomparable."

Ueland believed, as I do, that originality springs from
authenticity, and authenticity springs from inspiration
from our prayer for it. She believed in listening for guidance from higher realms. Walking, we clear our channels.
We hear our guidance clearly and without the friction of
our daily circumstances. As we pray "Please guide me,"
we are, in fact, guided. Ideas come to us, and later, as
we put them to the page, we have a comforting sense of
validity.

Ueland argues that using our creative powers makes
us healthy. She writes, "Why should we all use our creative power? Because there is nothing that makes people
so generous, joyful, lively, bold and compassionate, so in-
different to fighting and the accumulation of objects and
money."

Spiritual teacher Sonia Choquette agrees with Ueland
that writing brings health. She believes we strengthen
our soul whenever we write out our truth. "Behind every
word lies power," she writes, "whether you believe it or
not."

I say, believe it. As we write out our hopes, dreams,
and desires, we trigger the universe to act on our behalf.
We are, indeed, as Ueland states, "forever talked to by
God and his messengers."

Inspiration comes to us as we walk. Novelist John
Nichols, of *The Milagro Beanfield War* fame, walks daily.
So do I, and so does Natalie Goldberg. Ueland has this to
say about that: "I will tell you what I have learned myself:
for me, a long five- or six-mile walk helps. And one must
go alone and every day."

Emma Lively, writer and composer, walks daily. As she
walks, she daydreams. She experiences hunches, inklings,

If you want to change the world, pick up your pen and write.

—MARTIN LUTHER

and inspiration. Coming home, she sets her hand to the page, writing out melodies and scenes for her musicals. Lively believes what Ueland wrote: "Imagination needs noodling; long, inefficient happy idling; dawdling and puttering . . ."

I head out for my own walk, crisscrossing the mountain roads of Santa Fe as majestic hawks swoop above and dancer-like deer cross my path down below. Arriving home, pen to page, I write my first thought, and a second follows. Leaning into my ideas, I find my thoughts coming easily. I credit this to my walk. Unkinking my body, I have unkinked my mind.

THE DAILY QUOTA

Let me say it again: Morning Pages are three pages of longhand writing on eight and a half by eleven-inch paper. The first page and a half come easily. The second page and a half are more difficult, but contain pay dirt. Writing pages daily yields results. Now, I want to mention another equally valid regime: a daily quota of writing on your project.

As with Morning Pages, the first page and a half are easy, the second page and a half more difficult. The trick here is to write a set number of pages on your project, every day. I say three if you are writing a play or a movie, two if you are writing prose, which is more dense. Setting the bar low, at three pages or two, guarantees that you will be able to accomplish it. As your daily pages mount up, so will your self-esteem. Restless? Feeling you could do more? Resist the temptation. Slow and steady wins the day. Use the mantra "easy does it," reminding yourself that it means "easy accomplishes it." Your slow pace is actually fast. Ninety pages of a movie in a month, sixty pages of prose. Write daily, and feel the thrill of accomplishment. Take pride in your progress.

Take pride, too, in your creative upkeep. Writing daily, you are drawing heavily and steadily on your inner well. Take care to restock that well by a practice of regular Artist Dates. What are they again? An Artist Date is a solo, festive expedition to do something fun, something that enchants or interests you. Self-elected fun, an Artist Date refills your inner well. You have used images and ideas by writing. You replace images and ideas by Artist Dates. As a rule of thumb, one Artist Date weekly is sufficient. But if you feel your writing becoming more difficult and thin, then a second weekly date is the remedy.

If you wish to be a writer, write.

—EPICTETUS

As with Morning Pages, regularity is the key. As you meet your low and doable quota, your pride in your authorship will grow. Your identity as a working writer will become more secure. A feeling of faith and satisfaction will replace anxiety about your project. By keeping the bar low, your imagination will meet the daily challenge. Your flow of ideas will keep pace with your outflow.

"Julia, you're so productive," I am often told—sometimes with a touch of scolding. The unspoken question is, "How?"

"The key to productivity is regularity," I reply. And so I keep to my routine of Morning Pages, Artist Dates, and walks, and to my regime of hitting my daily quota. This book is being written slowly and steadily. The even pace promotes an even caliber of writing. A day at a time, I practice what I preach.

WHO CAN WRITE?

We have a mythology that tells us that writers—real writers—are an elite few. I'd like to challenge that mythology. It's my belief that all of us can write. It's just that so many of us are afraid to put pen to page. Fearful of being judged, fearful of looking foolish, we hang back.

"I'd love to write, but . . ." begins our litany of excuses.

"I'd love to write, but I have nothing to say." "I'd love to write, but I don't have the discipline." "I'd love to write, but I can't spell, can't punctuate . . ." "I'd love to write, but . . ."

But nothing. Just as we all can speak, we all can put words to the page. Some of us know this fact, and call ourselves writers. Others of us fear this fact. To them, the spoken word is one thing, and the written word another. Afraid to put their thoughts to the page, they freeze up. There is a way around this phenomenon, and that is the practice of Morning Pages.

Three pages of longhand writing that is not *really* writing, the pages teach us to move past our inner critic, that voice which tells us, "You can't write, not really."

Yes, we really can write, and the pages give us practice. The pages are for our eyes only. They are a safe place to vent, to dare, to dream, and, yes, to write.

Start writing, no matter what. The water does not flow until the faucet is turned on.

—LOUIS L'AMOUR

"Julia, I wrote Morning Pages and they made me a novelist," one practitioner told me. I'm not surprised. The pages unlock an inner door. Stepping through that door, we live our dreams. And many of us dream of being a writer.

"Julia, I always wanted to be a writer, and now I am one. I did Morning Pages and dared to write a book. This afternoon I did the photo shoot for the cover."

"Julia, I'm seventy years old and I just finished my first play."

Accolades like these come to me often. Writing Morning Pages frees the writer within. "I'd love to be a writer but . . ." is transformed to "I think I might be a writer and . . ." Our negative mythology around writing begins to fade in the face of our experience. "I may be a writer" starts to dissolve our skepticism. Morning Pages assure us that our emerging identity is valid. They witness our transformation from non-writer to writer. We begin to realize that writing, the act of writing, is what makes us a writer. Far from being an elite tribe from which we are excluded, writers are a generous tribe to which we now belong. The obstacles which loomed so large are now diminished. Non-spelling gives way to spellcheck. Punctuation yields to *The Elements of Style*.

"I think I may be a writer," we tell ourselves, at first tentatively, then with gathering strength. As our negative mythology fades away, we recognize our new identity. Our joy in putting pen to page supersedes our fear. Yes, we love to write.

PROTECTING YOUR INNER ARTIST

For the better part of three decades, we have heard talk of our "inner child"—so much talk, we're sick of it. Our inner child, we have been told, must be protected from wounding—or, once wounded, must be allowed to heal. So now I find myself adding one more voice to the chorus: protect your inner child, known for our purposes here as your inner writer.

Make no mistake: our inner writer *is* an inner youngster—a tender, vulnerable youngster. The part of us that creates is easily wounded, hurt by too much attention of the wrong kind. Vulnerable, open to feedback, it is also open to criticism. A careless critical arrow can pierce its heart. As we write, we have two separate and distinct personas: our inner writer and our inner adult. It falls to the latter to protect and defend the former. Insofar as it's possible, our adult creates a safe environment. There are several ways this is accomplished. Not surprisingly, the first is Morning Pages.

It is our adult self which makes the commitment and summons the discipline to write Morning Pages. That said, the pages are a safe arena for our writer to vent, to dream, to dare. Wounded by unjust criticism, our writer takes to the pages to complain and grieve. Writing out our pain, the writer feels seen and heard. Our adult self swings into action, soothing the wounded writer. Although it may not be sent, we write a letter to the editor in our own defense.

Pages give us a safety net. With pages in place, our writer finds resiliency. No matter what damning damage is leveled our way, pages tell us we will survive to write another day. They tell us we are strong enough not only to survive but to prevail. As we write out our grievances, we miniaturize them. We draw them to scale. Balanced against our commitment to write daily, they are small potatoes.

Our adult self chooses for our writer safe companions, those with generosity enough to applaud our work. Our adult self selects a posse of believing mirrors, those large enough to take us in and large enough to reflect back to us our strength and possibility. This is where our adult flexes its muscles of discernment. There is no room here for the jealous or the petty. Those are enemies to our writer, and our adult self sees them clearly for the foes that they are. The adult self is alert for snipers, those people who can't resist taking a potshot born out of envy and fear. I say "fear" because our writer can appear threatening. We may experience ourselves as small and vulnerable, but appear to the world at large as intimidating. Our candor, a great gift to the world, may loom as a threat. Snipers may try to take us down a notch, and this is where our adult musters our defense.

"You have a right to your opinion, a right to express yourself," our adult may weigh in in our defense. Defended, our writer rallies.

"I do have rights," it tells us, and the attack of the sniper is dismantled.

"You need a treat," our adult may advise us. Here we heed the advice, "Treating yourself like a precious object will make you strong." Spoiling yourself a little, devising festive adventures for your writer to enjoy, is one more layer of defense. We play, and experience the play of ideas. Your adult self caters to your inner youngster. An Artist Date builds strength. And so we see that our adult has many stratagems for safeguarding our writer. Alert to foes, most especially bullies, our adult stands firm.

"I am big enough and strong enough to withstand hostility," our writer comes to believe. Trusting our adult, our writer flourishes.

A ROOM OF ONE'S OWN

Virginia Woolf, that fine writer, stated her estimable opinion that in order to be a writer, one needed a room of one's own. Not wanting to quibble, I found myself differing. After all, many would-be writers lacked the means to have a room of their own. And so I proposed that what Virginia meant was that writers require privacy. That was an opinion I could second.

If writers needed privacy, I could devise a way to give it to them: Morning Pages. Personal, private, for no eyes but their own, Morning Pages gave writers a safe place to vent, a safe place to dream, a safe place to dare. With no prying eyes, Morning Pages became a place where we could be authentically, truly ourselves.

Being truly ourselves is a prerequisite of good writing. We are the origin of our work. When we are authentic, we are original. Our resulting work is original. Our thoughts are clear, and clarity springs from privacy.

I am a writer perhaps because I am not a talker.

—GWENDOLYN BROOKS

"A room of one's own" induces privacy, and so do Morning Pages. Taking pen to page upon awakening, we discover our thoughts and feelings. We write from an undefended place, as if we were alone in the solitude of our personal domain. Sequestered to ourself, our thoughts become far-ranging. We are free to ruminate on anything and everything. We become inspired.

Our inspiration is the fruit of our solitude. Left to our own devices, we discover a wealth of thoughts. We pursue inklings and ideas. We chase our mind with curiosity: What next?

Morning Pages open an inner portal. They put us in touch with a flow of creativity and insight that might otherwise elude us. As if we had closed a door, separating us from other concerns, the Morning Pages give us detachment. We are removed from the agendas of others. We strike out on our own path.

A room of one's own may be a luxury we can't afford, while a journal is affordable by all. As the pages mount up, so, too, does our autonomy. And that is what Virginia Woolf was driving at.

WRITING STATIONS

I'm sitting in my library, a large, square room with mountain views. I am seated in a large leather chair—my writing chair. The foursquare room lends itself to clear and logical thinking. It is for me a "writing station," a place where I am comfortable taking pen to page. All told, I have four writing stations in my house, each one unique in character. I migrate room to room, matching my mood to the station's character. The library station is for plain-spoken prose, the kind I am writing now. When I want to focus on clarity and service, I come to this room. My prose becomes straightforward: I say what I mean and I mean what I say. The writing done here is workmanlike, easily understood. I typically use this station in the afternoon, when I am brisk and awake.

A second writing station is the couch in my exercise room. It's not a comfortable couch, and so I use it to jot myself brief notes. I walk on my treadmill, get an idea, take to the couch, and write my idea out. I may interrupt my writing to make a phone call. This writing station favors terse communiqués. Unlike the library, which is comfortable, this station is for dashed-off notes, quick, before the couch causes a backache. I use this station for writing that can't wait. Not for here are long meandering passages; no, those are best saved for more comfortable surroundings, which brings us to writing station number three.

The loveseat in my living room is comfortable. It faces a large, square window framing my piñon tree and the mountains beyond. A squat lamp sits by its side, casting a warm glow. The writing that happens here is warm and expansive, more imaginative than the work done in the library. I can sit easily here for several hours. Writing long-hand, I fill page after page. One thought leads to the next. My comfortable station lends itself to ease. I write here almost without effort. The window holds daylight, then twilight, then night. I write of many moods, each one welcomed by my station. My writing is fluid, thought leading to thought as I free-associate idea to idea. Of all my writing stations, this one is my favorite. Time speeds past. This station makes writing deeply pleasurable. I need to rouse myself to go to writing station four.

My house is shaped like a giant horseshoe. Writing station four is cradled in its arms: an outdoor, fresh air station where poetry resides. This station is a pair of chairs facing onto a courtyard and a garden. When I sit here, I write flora and fauna reports, spotting a large cotton-tail nibbling on the greenery. And what is this? A sly lizard scooting across the flagstones. Inspiration comes, as M. C. Richards says, "through the window of irrelevance." I catch sight of a songbird trilling in the plum tree. Out of the corner of my eye, topics suggest themselves. My writing here speaks of nature. I am enchanted by a pass-ing butterfly. A hummingbird pays a visit. I record it all.

Stations one to four each serve a purpose. Their vari-ety keeps boredom at bay. I am productive and creative moving spot to spot, station to station. My writing takes many forms, and each locale calls writing forth. I *love* to write.

GROUNDING

The day is gray and chill. The sky is overcast, and still more large clouds loom on the horizon. Rain is in the offing. It's a good day to be tucked indoors. Without my daily walk, I am restless, and the little dog is restless too. The house is crowded with prayerful intentions. I take to the page, and put my prayers in writing. "Please guide me," I write, and then I listen.

Spiritual teachers tell us that it is important for us to be "in the now." In the precise present, we can find a sense of tranquility. Centered in the moment that we are in, we are able to hear spiritual guidance. There are few ways of centering ourselves better than writing.

A friend of mine is a newcomer to Morning Pages. "Julia," he called to tell me, "the pages make me feel so clear."

My friend had tried other forms of meditation only to abandon them because his thoughts felt scattered. A writer by trade, he had undertaken the Morning Pages reluctantly. "I already write," he told me.

"Just try them," I urged. And so, my friend undertook the pages against his better judgment. To his surprise, doing Morning Pages made his other "real" writing flow more easily.

"The pages prioritize your day," I explained. "They keep you grounded because they keep you from being swept up in other people's agendas."

I recently gave a talk at a large bookstore. The venue was jammed with seekers. Faced with a large audience, I couldn't resist teaching the value of Morning Pages. When I finished my talk, a man approached me.

"I want to thank you for a quarter century of Morning Pages," he said. "In all that time I've missed only one day, and that was the day I had quadruple bypass surgery."

Faced with such a testimonial, I basked for a moment in the man's spiritual energy. He was relaxed and happy, although eager to share his report. Clearly he felt the pages had served him well.

"I used to do pages," another participant told me, "and listening to you, I feel I should do pages again. They made a tremendous difference in my life. I undertook a memoir at their urging. I self-published it, and now it's been picked up by a press. They're interested in my second book, they tell me, but I am stymied. Do you think pages would be a help?"

"Yes, I do. Pages are always a help."

Natalie Goldberg, a Zen Buddhist, practices mindfulness. She puts her pen to the page and records her precise surroundings and mood. She calls this "writing practice," and she cautions practitioners not to let themselves be "thrown away" by what they discover. She herself has stuck resolutely to the page, detailing her turbulent emotions during a yearlong battle with leukemia. Victorious, finally, over her cancer, she writes of her jubilant relief. Her writing has served to anchor her. Of course it has. Writing is grounding.

I recently met a young woman named Fiona. She rushed to my side in a bookstore. "I just want to thank you," she said. "I did Morning Pages and the pages nudged me to write a book. This afternoon I did a photo shoot for the book's cover. I feel that without Morning Pages, I would never have dared to write a book. Thank you so much."

Morning Pages, as Fiona discovered, ground us. Grounded, we are led—one step at a time—to take risks. The pages serve as a witness and confidante. The events of our life may not be as turbulent and troublesome as Natalie's cancer, but all the circumstances of our lives deserve metabolizing, and that is what the pages do.

As we embrace the practice of putting pen to page, we embrace our many moods. Accepting our moods, we become intimate with ourself and with our Higher Power. We experience a spiritual connection, and that connection brings us grounding—and peace.

EXPANSION

A dozen fat pink roses grace my living room coffee table. The blooms are gigantic, and bursting with beauty. Their scent wafts softly on the air. The roses are four days old and holding. Every time I pass the table, I dip my head to take in their aroma. The roses smell sweet, heavy, and dusty. They are an aphrodisiac. I breathe them in, and, enchanted, I take to the page and gladly write of the spell they cast. I daydream of a rose garden stretching for miles. My bouquet unlocks an inner door for inspiration.

Inspiration comes of working every day.

—CHARLES
BAUDELAIRE

Our writing mythology tells us that we need to go to Paris—or perhaps Morocco—to get inspired, but this is not the case. We can become inspired by our daily lives. As we write Morning Pages, we connect to the many details—like the roses—that spell inspiration and expansion. Writing our daily pages, we find ourselves interested by the flow of our own lives. Many small details capture our attention. We do not need high drama or foreign locale high stakes. A bouquet of roses, or lilies, or even daisies, can turn the gears of inspiration.

"Julia, my life is boring," we may say before we begin pages, but our lives are not boring, as we soon learn. As a rule, it takes but a few weeks to become fascinated with our own daily progression, as artists and indeed as people. Morning Pages coax us into greater creativity. They are a profound exercise in risk-taking. Each day, as we risk putting our thoughts on the page, is an act of daring.

The pages, in turn, invite more daring. We realize that we are not trapped in lackluster lives. We have many small "choice points" where we can choose to either expand or contract. Expansion is the order of the day.

"What should I do next?" we ask in our pages, and the answers may often surprise us. I had been writing pages for fifteen years when they suggested I would "soon be writing radiant songs." Raised to believe myself nonmusical, coming from a highly musical family, I brushed aside the suggestion, saying to myself, "Surely if I were musical, I would know it by now." But in response to my repeated questioning, "What shall I do next?" the pages repeated themselves: "You will be writing radiant songs."

I was visiting a girlfriend in Boulder, Colorado, and I told her about the pages' suggestion, and my deeply held skepticism that I was not musical. She listened patiently, and then suggested that I go sit by a mountain creek and meditate. I found a large boulder near the creek and listened to the rippling water. Suddenly, I "heard" both lyrics and music. I ran up the mountain to my friend, and said, "Listen to this! I think it's a song!" It *was* a song, a radiant song. The pages had nudged me to expand.

When I travel to teach, I hear many similar stories. People will say, "Julia, the pages urged me to write a book, and here it is." Or, "The pages urged me to start a radio show, or enter my art in a juried show." Always, the risks urged by the pages seem at first to be impossible, too expansive, but after their repeated suggestions, the risks seem smaller somehow, more doable. A page at a time, a step at a time, we expand. Practitioners progress from exclaiming, "Oh, I couldn't do that!" to "Maybe I could try," and, finally, to "I can't believe it; I've done it!"

Writing Morning Pages, my friend Ed, like Elizabeth Gilbert, discovered a hunger for all things Italian. At first he thought, "I'm too old to learn a foreign language," but then he began studying "beginner's Italian." After a few months, he had a working knowledge of everyday Italian. He could order food and ask directions. An avid bicyclist, he noted a notice at his bike shop of an Italian bicycle tour. Setting aside his reservations—again, "I'm too old"—he phoned the number on the card. He learned that there were many bikers in his age bracket. And so, dubious but excited, he signed up for the tour. His Morning Pages assured him he was taking a risk that would bring him great pleasure. He had moved from the sidelines into a stream of adventure. His "boring" life was now filled with excitement.

Yes, Morning Pages had lured him into an expanded life. Ed's story is familiar to me. Student after student has testified that the consistent use of Morning Pages is a portable and reliable source of expansion. They dare on the page, then they dare in life.

Like my roses, my pages dare me to dream.

WRITING AS A SPIRITUAL PATH

Although we tend to think of writing in secular terms, it is actually a spiritual path. We can consciously invite spiritual guidance. A simple prayer is relevant: "Okay, God, you take care of the quality, I'll take care of the quantity." When I was first told this prayer, I thought it was far-fetched. I had trouble believing that the spirit of the universe could take an interest in my prose. But as I retired from my ego's need to be a brilliant author, my writing became more clear. No longer aimed at being impressive and brilliant, it aimed instead to be forthright. I came to believe that "creator" was another word for "artist." I trusted the Great Artist—in the words of Dylan Thomas, "the force that through the green fuse drives the flower." I tried to think of myself like a flower, mysteriously blooming. I tried to be humbly obedient. I came to believe that honesty and authenticity could capture my reader's faith.

Writing Morning Pages is like sending a telegram to the universe. We give our precise coordinates: here, and how, I am. The universe, in response, acts on our behalf. Although we may not call it that, we have sent a prayer. Implicit in each day's pages is the request "Please help me," and the universe does.

Writing pages, we dare to mention our dreams. The universe acts on those dreams, giving us what we need, if not what we want. At their root, Morning Pages are a prayer—a prayer of petition. We ask the universe for our dreams, wants, and needs, and the universe complies with our requests. We are met more than halfway by a benevolent something that we may hesitate to call God.

Although we may be reluctant to name it, spirituality is afoot. Our pages symbolize our willingness to talk to— and hear from—God. Writing pages, we swing open an inner door. In our imagination, we read an inscription: "This is the way to a faith that works."

Morning Pages, too, "work." As we clarify on the page our yearnings, those yearnings begin to be met. As one practitioner told me, "I'm a Jew and an atheist, hardly your target audience, but pages work for me."

What do we mean by "pages work"? What we are talking about is nothing less than a spiritual awakening. Our whole attitude and outlook upon life shifts. Where before, the world was forbidding, it comes now to be benevolent. We meet with ease situations that used to baffle us. Over time, we recognize that God is doing for us what we could not do for ourselves.

Are these extravagant promises? I don't think so. They are being fulfilled among us, sometimes quickly, sometimes slowly. They always materialize as we do the work of writing pages.

Whether we conceive of pages as putting us in touch with a benevolent something, or we think that pages are themselves that something, matters little. What counts is the daily practice: a form of meditation as well as prayer.

Morning Pages are a two-way street. We "send" and then we "receive." Ideas come to us—thoughts, intuition, inklings. We are guided and led, led forward carefully and well. I recently heard from a man who has been doing Morning Pages for twenty-two years. He is an atheist, and pages themselves are his higher power. He has written thirteen movies, leading me to tell him, "You don't believe in God, but God clearly believes in you." Increased productivity is a common fruit of Morning Pages. As we work with the pages, we become more bold, taking risks as the pages urge, moving from project to project without excruciating pauses in between. As we learn to doubt our doubts, we expand, becoming larger and braver. Pages give us a safety net. Our risks, once seeming too large, become smaller. After all, the pages catch us if we fall. They partner us. Like circus acrobats, we are expertly "caught." When used in conjunction with Artist Dates, Morning Pages promote synchronicity. We are increasingly in the right place at the right time. Our "luck" improves as we come to count on it. Morning Pages yield a spiritual path. We become more surefooted as we write. We speak to the universe, and it answers.

When we begin writing with where we are and how we feel in our Morning Pages, we are actually formulating a prayer. We are sending a telegram to the universe that says, "This is my precise place and these are my precise feelings. Can you help me?" As we delineate our position, we are sending an SOS. We are saying exactly what we feel, and that is an invitation to the universe to intervene on our behalf. Writing on our creative projects later in the day, the same philosophy applies.

Ours is a secular time, and we often fail to realize the power and potency of the written word as prayer. Putting pen to the page, listening for inspiration, we are uttering

Writing is prayer.

—FRANZ KAFKA

the perennial artist's prayer, "Please help me." It matters less sometimes what we write than that we write at all. Our words lead us to authenticity, just as authenticity leads us to our words. As we describe our state with specificity, we are given the gift of humility, and from humility, great art is born. Consider the Mona Lisa: the precise rendering of an enigmatic smile. Writing carefully, we, too, render the enigma that is the human condition. Great art is born from the prayer, "Please help me render what I see and what I hear."

My secular friends are astonished, and even offended by my use of prayer in writing. "Prayer works," I tell them, and, "As a working writer, I use anything that works."

"But Julia!" they exclaim, "Isn't that cheating?" They make writing sound like a circus trick that must be mastered.

Once upon a time, I tell them, everyone prayed. The inspiration for art routinely was ascribed to a higher power. In these modern times, we are reluctant to name God as our collaborator—and yet that is the experience of artists through the ages. As Brahms remarked, "Straightaway the ideas flow into me, directly from God." As William Blake remarked, "Not I, but the holy spirit does the work."

Artists of the ages have spoken of the divine origin of "their" ideas. Composers in particular speak of the "muse" in music. But all artists experience the spark of the divine. When we write humbly, we invite a flow of ideas not commonly our own. Listening to the thread of inspiration that leads us from one idea to the next, we often experience a sense of awe. It is as though we are fitting together a celestial puzzle, and as we place each thought on the page, we begin to see the form of what wants to be born. The experience of such inspiration is essentially an experience of grace. Divine ideas enter our thoughts. We take them *down,* but they lift us *up.*

Writing a poem, I often experience wonder as the final line twists into view. Some of my finest writing comes as a sort of celestial joke. I find myself thinking, "Oh! That's what they were up to!" By "they," I mean what I call "higher forces." As I write, I find myself guided.

In days of yore, artists routinely cited celestial inspiration filling their work. In modern times, we speak less freely of the divine, yet its inspiration remains real, if only we open our hearts to it. As we ask the universe to lead us, we are led carefully and well. Many an artist, in a candid moment, will speak of the surprise that comes to them in their art. The brilliant landscape painter Jamie Kirkland says, "My paintings never turn out like they are in my head. Instead, they surprise me."

TASKS

1. Morning Pages: Every morning, set your alarm thirty minutes early and write, longhand, three eight and a half by eleven-inch pages about anything and everything that comes to mind. I always say I would never stand between anyone and their morning coffee, but try to get to the page as quickly as possible—don't spend forty-five minutes brewing the perfect cup. The faster you get to the page, the better the pages will work for you. Avoid the phone, computer, and email until you have finished your pages. They will act as windshield wipers, clearing away what stands between you and your day.

2. Artist Date: Once a week, block out approximately two hours to take your inner writer on a solo adventure. It need not be expensive; the point is that you are spending one-on-one time with your artist to do something festive and out of the ordinary. This is a tool of expansion. Used in conjunction

with Morning Pages, you will find yourself in a flow of happy coincidences and good luck—which I like to call synchronicity. The Artist Date appears to take time, but it gives back energy and inspiration. Allow yourself to promise this date to your inner writer—and keep it.

3. Walks: Twice a week, or more often if you'd like to, take yourself on a solo, phone-free, dog-free, friend-free, twenty-minute walk. You may wish to walk out with a question—it is likely you will return with an answer. Walks will help you to metabolize this process, as well as provide inspiration and clarity in your writing.

4. The Daily Quota: Choose a low, doable daily quota for your writing project. (For screenplays, I usually suggest three pages a day; for prose, two.) Choose a quota that is low enough that it feels easily within reach on a daily basis. In addition to writing your Morning Pages, you will hit your daily quota on your writing project every day.

5. Writing Stations: Choose a few locations in your house or in your neighborhood where you can write. It may be a favorite chair or corner of a table; it may be your home office; it may be a nearby coffee shop. The important point is that you find these locations comfortable and enticing to write.

CHECK IN

1. How many days did you do your Morning Pages this week? Are you able to get to them quickly and do them without interruption or distraction?

2. Did you take your Artist Date? What was it? How was it? Did you experience synchronicity, optimism, or a sense of a benevolent higher power? All three?

3. Did you take your walks? Are you able to do them alone and without distraction? Did you try walking out with a question and seeing if you returned home with an answer?

4. Did you hit your daily quota? How many pages are you into your project? Do you feel a sense of excitement as you watch your page count building?

BEGIN WHERE YOU ARE

This week, you will establish habits and methods that will get you into consistent motion on your project. The essays of this week aim to help build routines that will allow your page count to grow in both a gentle and rapid fashion. We will address common stumbling blocks—and ways to evade them—as you invite your writing to be a daily, manageable, and enjoyable part of your life.

BEGIN WHERE YOU ARE

"If only I could begin," I am often told by would-be writers who can't get started.

"I know that if I could just begin, I'd be in good shape. But I can't seem to find my way in."

Begin at the beginning, I tell such writers, but they often complain, "I don't know the beginning." And so, I say, start where you are.

"But that seems so boring."

Where you are is not boring, I protest. It's the start of something grand. Let us say you are seated at your desk, looking out the window. A perfectly fine piece of writing might begin, "I'm seated at my desk, looking out the window." This first thought leads to a second. A thought at a time, a sentence at a time, the page fills.

I am sitting in my dining room, which features a crystal chandelier. As the sky outside darkens I switch on the light. Peering out the window, I see the great lopsided moon rising over the mountains. Tomorrow it will be

I write to find out what I'm talking about.

—EDWARD ALBEE

full, but tonight it is full enough. Its slivery light is phosphorescent. When Lily ventures outside, her coat glows in the dark.

It is a relief to be writing. With every word a tiny droplet of anxiety falls away. It feels good to put pen to page. I find myself writing late into the evening. Detail by detail, my life takes shape on the page. My psyche is soothed by the act of writing. I find myself hoping to convey my joy. Writing puts my world in order. Words are medicine—each one a balm strengthening my sense of well-being. I *love* to write.

LAYING TRACK

It's a quiet evening, ideal for writing. My phone has not rung, and I myself have made no calls. The essay that I have in mind is an important one, detailing a major writing "trick." I approach it with special care, wanting it to be persuasive. And so, here we go. I wish there were a classier way of saying it, but there is not. What I am talking about is laying track. What does it mean to "lay track"? It means to go from point A to point B without concern that we are taking the very best route. Laying track comes from the days when railroads were laid coast to coast, requiring a certain number of miles laid daily. Every day, a certain amount of track—a certain distance—needed to be covered. And so, the workers put down ties and rails until they reached their daily quota.

As writers, we can take a cue from this. We want to get from A to B to C, and so on through the alphabet, by small increments—our own daily quota.

In laying track, we are laying down a rough draft. It can be fixed later. Rough drafts should be exactly that: rough. Our perfectionist loathes this fact, but never mind. Later, when we retrace the distance laid, we can correct errors.

Tracing back over our route, we often find we have come very close to laying out a perfect draft. We do not need to fix much. The work seems to have an intelligence of its own. Let us say we are writing a mystery. We lay track a scene at a time, writing what occurs to us, not demanding to know why. When I was writing a mystery, on page seventeen, for no apparent reason, there was a gun on the table. The writing said, "Put a gun on the table," and so I did. I didn't know why, but I knew to obey. On page ninety-seven, that gun was used in self-defense. I have learned that all it takes is the courage to put on the page what we "hear."

Now let us say we are writing a love story. On page thirteen, the lovers meet. On page sixty-seven, the lovers kiss. The intervening pages detail their attraction, bit by bit. Whether writing a screenplay or writing a novel, we need to trust the native intelligence of the work at hand. The work has a shape, which it will tell us if we are open to it. Listening for the direction that the work intends to take gives us great originality. We lay down the track as it is "told" to us. By not second-guessing our ideas, we find ourselves writing freely and with authenticity.

When I got sober at age twenty-nine, I had already had a successful writing career. But I found myself tormented by what I perceived as the demands of my craft. I wrote and rewrote, laboring to meet my ego's demand that every sentence be exactly right. Imagine my shock and resistance when, newly sober, I was told to let a higher power write through me.

"What if it doesn't want to?" I immediately objected.

"Just try it," I was advised.

And so, I struck my bargain. ("Okay, God, you take care of the quality, I'll take care of the quantity.") Over my ego's objections, I began to write freely. A scene at a time, I wrote what wanted to come next. My ego didn't like it, but my spirit did. I was obedient to my hunches.

My writing improved. Without straining to be clever, my craft became less crafty. Without trying to be brilliant, I found myself more clearly communicative. Other people remarked favorably on the clarity of my writing. I discovered when I finished a rough draft that there was very little "rough" about it. Laying track worked. The writing had a mind of its own, and a smart mind at that. I need only to obediently write my daily quota, nothing more.

Laying track, the trick is to keep moving gently forward. Each day's quota builds on the previous day. And so we write our first draft straight through, without rewriting. Over my many years of writing, I have learned that the writing itself has wisdom. If I simply write down the ideas as they come to me, the ideas themselves will have a form. By laying daily track, I discover it, rather than invent it.

"But Julia," my students sometimes say, "you make it sound so easy."

Laying track *is* easy, I tell them. The ego hates this fact. I tell my students, all it takes is the humility to surrender control and write what you "hear." As promised to me many years ago, the higher power will write through you. You write without rewriting.

Get it down. Take chances. It may be bad, but it's the only way you can do anything good.

—WILLIAM FAULKNER

FIRST THOUGHTS

Tonight is a full moon, but thick clouds obscure the silvery disc. Lily is restless, perhaps feeling the full moon if not seeing it. I put pen to page and write that I am missing the moon. I have lived in Santa Fe for ten years now, and I have come to love the great bright moon clearing the mountains.

Lily's dog yard contains juniper trees and piñon. They are ordinarily washed silver by the light of the moon. Tonight, the dog yard is filled with shadows. Lily doesn't venture outside. Instead, she perches on the arm of my writing chair. She wants to play "grab the pen."

This is a book on writing, and so it must demonstrate what it teaches. And so I begin with the dimmed moon. Too often, when we sit down to write, we reject our initial idea. We rack our brains for something better. But long experience has shown me that my first idea is often my best idea. Writing, after all, is not meant to be torture. It helps to think of writing as a gentler process. First things first, a coaxing forward of ideas rather than a flailing forward of our thoughts. And so, we begin at the beginning: our first thought leads to our second, our second to our third, and so on.

A sense of direction is helpful here. When we write Morning Pages, we jot *down* our ideas. We do not strive to "think them up." We "hear" an idea, and we write it out. This "dictation" is done without strain. After all, the pages are private. So we need not strive to be smarter or more organized. You put in whatever strikes your fancy. When your writing is freed of the need to be perfect, it is often astonishing how close to perfect it becomes.

Writing my book *The Artist's Way,* I wrote essay after essay beginning with first thoughts. First thoughts led the way to further thoughts, and further thoughts led the way to further still. Arguably, *The Artist's Way* is an entire book built on first thoughts. First thoughts led the way.

The act of writing gives self-esteem. I set a low, manageable quotient and aim for that. Two pages a day is the amount of writing I can comfortably accomplish on a nonfiction book. A steady, even pace is what is called for.

"Julia, you are so productive," I am sometimes told. I hear this compliment to mean, "How do you do it?" How I do it is by doing it. I discount my mood and simply go to work.

"Julia, you've written so much," I am sometimes told.

There is something delicious about writing the first words of a story. You never quite know where they'll take you.

—BEATRIX POTTER

I hear this compliment to mean, "For you it must be easy." My writing is not easy, but it is practiced.

What we are talking about here is faith. It takes an act of faith to trust our first thoughts. We sit down to write, and we ask, "Where shall I begin?" The question provokes an answer. That answer may strike us as farfetched, but experience has shown me it is accurate.

I recently sat down to write a play. "Where shall I begin?" I asked, and I "heard," "Begin with songbirds." This answer felt muddy to me—too soft for my hard-hitting characters. Yet, trained by long years of experience, I found myself obedient. I opened my play with the line, "Listen. Aren't they lovely?" My hero had a soft spot: his love of the musicality of birds. Trusting my first thought, I found my character more human. My first thought was a necessary corrective to my intellectual plan. By trusting my first thought, I was given a tenderhearted hero, not at all the caustic, wheelchair-bound person I had envisioned.

"I kept waiting for resentment, bitterness, and hatred," a reader remarked. "Instead, I found courage."

Writing, teaching, I have learned to follow my first impulse. The wisdom contained in first thoughts is often revealed later. In my play, the songbirds set up a complex imagery. "Listen. Aren't they lovely?" opened an inner door.

WHAT TO WRITE

It's a calm day: pale blue sky, wispy white clouds. I'm at writing station number three, looking out the large window at the mountains. I have been writing slowly but steadily. I've paused, tinkered at my tiny piano, writing out a song. The break did me good and now I'm ready to write again. But what to write about? I've done my Morning Pages, and I look to them for a topic. I find that they skitter topic to topic. I look for one topic more pressing than the others, and I find it. I will write about that. This topic has more "juice" than the others. Scanning my Morning Pages, I feel its voltage. It kicks over a gear that says, "Now let's write."

I love to write, and so I take to the page eagerly. My writing explores my mind. Pen to page, I find out what I think. Writing brings clarity, and clarity brings satisfaction. I love the process of learning my own mind.

A topic at a time, egged on by curiosity, I write my thoughts. If no topic suggests itself, I lace up my shoes and go for a walk. Walking, I find that topics come to me. I mull them over a footfall at a time. Coming home, I take pen to page. It's a rarity that no topic seizes my attention.

On the occasions when I experience no topic, I strive not to panic over my blank slate. I recognize that it's simply time to take an Artist Date, restocking my inner well. I try to choose something delectable. I want to feel enchantment, even glee. My favorite Artist Date is a visit to the pet store that houses George, an enormous bunny. I have permission to pet George, and I do so, to his joy and mine. Going home, I find myself ready to write. Several topics abound and I choose among them, like picking one flower from a bouquet. Writing leads to writing. One topic leads to the next. What I write matters, but *that* I write matters more.

WRITING SCHEDULES

I begin each day by writing Morning Pages. Pen to page, I record my mood and the weather—often tied together. Take this morning: I woke with a start. It was still dark. Storm clouds rolled down from the mountains. I felt anxious, weather pending. The Morning Pages were an uphill climb, a task I set for myself, the first stop on my writing schedule. I recorded my anxiety, my dark mood matching the day. Tomorrow might be sunny, brightening my mood and what I put to the page. Daily pages keep a record of my life. I pray on the page, writing out my intentions. I ask for guidance, and record what I am told. Pages done, it's time for breakfast—oatmeal, most mornings—a meal that fortifies my day. It takes energy to write. When I am working on a project, it comes next, the second stop on my writing schedule. Curled on my living room love seat, I touch pen to paper. I will write for an hour, perhaps two. On those rare days when I do not write, I become crabby—restless, irritable, and discontent—all symptoms of my need to write. I do not schedule my writing day by the clock, rather, I schedule it by my mood.

Sunny days I write soon; cloudy days I procrastinate, trying my hand at a poem before setting to work on my project. On this book, I am averaging three pages daily; a brief essay's worth. Some days, I have an appetite for further work, and so I have a third stop on my writing schedule, but it comes later in the day. First, I will walk a mile or so. Next I will nap. Waking in the late afternoon, I've fooled my writer into a second wind. I retreat to the library, curl in my writing chair, and ask myself, "Now what?" The "what" that comes is a further essay. I write rapidly, knowing that across town, my friend Natalie Goldberg is also writing. Like me, she writes at all hours, scheduling her writing by her itch to write.

Now it is twilight. My friend, the novelist John Nichols, is ready to begin his writing "day." He writes each day at dusk, working often until the wee hours. More disciplined than I, he schedules his writing by the clock. Dinner hour finds him at his desk. The afternoon that I spend writing, he hikes a small mountain. Walking primes his pump and leaves him ready to create.

Remember to get the weather in your damn book—weather is very important.

—ERNEST HEMINGWAY

Nick Kapustinsky, poet-actor-writer, rises each day to Morning Pages. But then his workday takes over, and he has no more time to write. Instead, as he passes through his day, he jots notes on his phone. "This was interesting . . . this was hard . . ." At night, he schedules time to write, hours when he reviews his day's notes, looking for what to write about. Like Nichols, he is a climber. When he shoehorns a hike into his already busy day, he carries with him a notebook. "You never know when inspiration will strike," he says. And, notebook in hand, he is prepared. His hikes are strenuous, and his poems are likewise muscular, lean, and sinewy. He writes daily every evening, when his experience is fresh.

Emma Lively, another practitioner of Morning Pages, credits them with giving her the ability to write anytime, anywhere. A composer and lyricist, she alternates songwriting with prose. She has been my editor on four books, and she jostles her writing schedule to fit around mine. "Anytime, anywhere" gives her quite a daily workout.

As these writers show, writing schedules are a matter of matching temperament to the task at hand. Whether set by mood, or on the clock, regularity is key. Writing is flexible, but it thrives on routine. Natalie, John, Nick, Emma—all set their schedule to match as individuals. Like me, they love to write, and write, they do.

GRABBING TIME

It's twilight. I am meeting friends in half an hour, and it would be easy to say there's not enough time to write. But I have learned that writing requires the barest sliver of time, and so here I am, taking pen to page, writing about an important writer's trick, which I am practicing: grabbing time.

"All I need in order to write more is to have more time. Why, if I had a year off, I'd be able to write a novel."

The best time for planning a book is while you're doing the dishes.

—AGATHA CHRISTIE

How many times I have heard this sentiment. One of our most damaging myths about writing is that it takes great swaths of uninterrupted time. I have been writing since I was eighteen, and I have never found a great swath of time. Instead, I found snippets. I found that writing could be done quickly. All that was necessary was to "grab" the time I actually had.

My inner writer is easily bribed. "Just write for twenty minutes, and then I'll give you a treat," I often say. Of course, twenty minutes often leads to forty, but even when it is kept to twenty, I find I am able to lay a surprising amount of track. The trick, of course, is to write and not rewrite. When Mark Bryan and I were writing *Money Drunk, Money Sober,* we often wrote in short twenty-minute spurts. Reading the book later, I found that it read smoothly, as one verse of writing led the way to another. At the risk of sounding like a fanatic, I want to point out again that the practice of Morning Pages trains us to write quickly, moving from topic to topic and thought to thought. Both Mark and I were practitioners of Morning Pages. Our practice served us well. We grabbed for time in our busy lives and found we had "enough time" for an entire book. But the practice of grabbing time must be tried to be believed.

Regina is a screenwriter, and she found herself victimized by the "time lie." Forty pages into a script, she had eighty pages to go, but couldn't find time to write.

"Just dash to the page," I told her. "Write what comes to mind, and stop second-guessing yourself. Pretend you are writing Morning Pages. Your first thoughts are often your best thoughts," I explained. "Just try trusting them."

Regina protested, "My life is already overcrowded. Writing seems like one more job. You make writing seem doable. I don't have time to write."

"You do have time. It is doable," I told her. "We want to make it hard, and believe that we need a great deal of time. And believing that we need a great deal of time is one of our primary writer's blocks. You're addicted to procrastination," I told Regina. "When you procrastinate, thinking your ideas over and over again, you do need a lot of time to write. Anyone can find twenty minutes," I coaxed her. "Just try writing down your first thought."

"Oh, all right," Regina relented. "I'll try it."

She did try it.

"I can't believe how much time I wasted," exclaimed Regina a scant month later. She was now "hooked" on the notion of grabbing time. She explained, "It wasn't that I didn't have time. It was that I was stalling. But now, twenty minutes at a time, I am making a lot of progress— and I am feeling pretty good about what I am producing!"

As Regina learned, grabbing time is a tool for dismantling perfectionism. When we write quickly, we write freely, and writing freely, we lay track.

Carl was a highly successful lawyer who dreamed of writing.

"But I just don't have the time," he complained to me. "I'm buried in my job."

"Of course you have the time," I told him, and like Regina, I urged him to try grabbing twenty minutes.

"I'd think that wouldn't be enough to accomplish anything worthwhile." Carl's tone was dejected. I could hear how painfully he wanted to write.

"One way to find out?" I offered. I asked him to experiment and record the results.

"Maybe I can grab twenty minutes on my lunch hour," Carl offered.

"Yes," I said, "or on your commuter train home." I told him about novelist Scott Turow, who used his commuter ride to write a best-selling book.

The trick is to simply "drop down the well," trusting that the flow of creative ideas is always running just below the surface of everyday life. Carl found that when he grabbed only twenty minutes, he was able to write twice daily; once at lunch and once as his train carried him home.

"I hate to say this, but I'm making up for the years I was not writing, and my wife says that my temperament has improved."

No surprise, really, that Carl is more cheerful. A writer who is writing is always more cheerful than a writer who is blocked. Both Regina and Carl now swear by the trick of "grabbing time."

"I've written seventy pages in twenty-minute increments," says Regina, "and I have learned that to be productive, all one needs to do is to set aside skepticism and grab for time."

SPIRITUAL CHIROPRACTIC

Morning Pages prioritize the day. "First things first," they teach. Moving through the day a "jump" at a time, we find ourselves doing "the next right thing." There is no quibbling. There is little procrastination. Instead, we move smoothly from one thing to the next. Rather than arguing, we take the next jump as it looms before us. We are like steeple chasers taking hurdle after hurdle, fence after fence.

Although pages take time to execute, they save us time throughout the day. We are no longer taking "mental cigarette breaks" while we ponder what to do next. Now we know what's next: the next right thing. With the help of pages, we sort the trivial from the important. The trivial falls to one side as we focus on what really matters. We don't fritter time away on the inconsequential. No, with pages in place we have a sense of our priorities.

I have often called Morning Pages a "radical codependency withdrawal." By that I mean we withdraw our energies into our own core. We are no longer swept away by the agendas of others. We stick to our own. We no longer squander our creativity "people pleasing" others. Instead, we learn to please ourselves, placing our needs and wants ahead of theirs. We are often astonished by the sheer amount of energy that comes bounding back to us. This energy is ours to do with what we please. For many of us, this is a novel experience. We are so accustomed to helping others that it can feel scary, even risky, to help ourselves.

Morning Pages teach us that we matter. They perform spiritual chiropractic, moving us into alignment with our own dreams, hopes, and goals. A page at a time, we move toward our "true north" as our authentic desires cue us in to action on our own behalf. We find that in a day we face many "choice points" where we can choose to act in our own best interests. Morning Pages promote a healthy selfishness. For many of us, this is radical behavior.

"What do I want? What are my goals?" are questions that we learn to ask ourselves. When we find ourselves straying from our heart's desires, we learn to catch ourselves and correct our course. Increasingly, we learn to fire "the arrow of desire." We aim for what we truly want, feeling the thrill of satisfaction as we score a bull's-eye. And again, the next right thing becomes increasingly apparent. We aim with our heart and we hit the mark.

PERFECTIONISM

When I teach, I ask a simple question: How many of you feel you have an issue with perfectionism? Hands shoot into the air. Nearly everybody has an issue with perfectionism.

Rough drafts should be rough, but we seldom give ourselves permission to write that way. Instead, we aim for perfection. We want our rough drafts to be polished.

This is too bad, for perfectionism is the enemy of art: it stifles the creative impulse. Rather than allowing ourselves freedom, we demand instead a suffocating standard that leaves no room for error. Searching for the precise right word, we find it difficult to write at all. We are hamstrung by our icy demands. Take now: the mountain peaks are rosy at sunset. Rather than write this plain fact, we struggle to describe the peaks perfectly. The peaks are lit by sunset. But is "lit" the word we want? Perhaps "illuminated" would be better. Perhaps not. We argue with ourselves as the sun sinks deeper and the peaks fade to black. Yes, perfectionism is the enemy of creativity, the enemy of freedom, the enemy of a full day's work.

Pegi, a journalist, found herself writing—and rewriting—her assignment. As her deadline loomed, her anxiety increased, and her perfectionism sharpened its claws.

"I have to finish," Pegi yelped, "but I'm stuck." She found herself cornered by her perfectionism. I suggested she try an Artist's Way tool. Numbering from one to five, writing quickly, she finished the phrase, "If I didn't have to say it perfectly, I'd say . . ." She was able to state clearly what she wanted to write.

"The trick is getting past your critic," I told her. "Speed helps."

I explained that we all have an inner critic, a kind of schoolyard bully who will diminish our efforts—usually in a less than sophisticated way. She laughed with recognition.

"This is the voice in my head that says, 'You're boring. You're dumb,'" she said. "And you're right. I'd like to tell it to just buzz off."

"Humor helps," I told her. She laughed aloud as her perfectionism melted.

"Why, my critic seems foolish," she exclaimed. "I found myself saying 'nothing is perfect, so leave me alone.'"

To Pegi's surprise, her critic backed down.

"My critic is nothing but a bully," she said, "and everyone knows when you stand up to a bully, it backs down."

I told Pegi her perfectionism was no longer running the show.

"You're right," she told me, "and dismantling it now seems simple. Thanks for the tool."

Our critic may speak up, telling us our ideas are hackneyed. But we learn to speak back to our critic, saying, "Thank you for sharing, but I think I'll just keep writing."

Our critic *is* like a schoolyard bully; as we stand up to it, its power is diminished, just as a bully backs down when confronted.

If you are in difficulties with a book, try the element of surprise: attack it at an hour when it isn't expecting it.

—H. G. WELLS

THE INNER CRITIC

The day is bright and sunny. I am in my living room with its mountain views. Clouds wrap the summit. But what's this? My writing is interrupted by the voice of my inner critic.

"Another weather report. How boring," he declares.

"Shush," I say, and keep on writing. My critic, as I've written before, is named Nigel. In my imagination, Nigel is a British interior decorator. His aesthetics always supersede my own.

"Don't write about the weather," Nigel chides. "I'm telling you, no one cares."

"But it's beautiful," I object.

"Romantic nonsense," Nigel protests.

I hush him again, although I recognize that with him, there is no winning.

When I wrote *The Artist's Way,* Nigel told me no one would want to read it. That book has now sold more than five million copies, but Nigel continues to insist that its popularity is a fluke. When I wrote my second book, *The Vein of Gold*, Nigel told me it was boring. I finished the book anyway, and am frequently told by readers that the book was "a great adventure" for them. My third book found Nigel telling me my ideas were hackneyed and my prose style lumpish. I didn't think it was true, but it scared me.

That became the pattern: Nigel would tell me something terrifying about each new book and I would become frightened that Nigel was right. Finishing the books became an uphill task. Several years ago, I wrote a book which provoked Nigel into fury. Every day when I worked on the project, Nigel would weigh in with vicious remarks. "This book is terrible, no good at all, useless," Nigel's comments ran. Tutored by my Morning Pages, I kept on writing, and Nigel kept on disparaging my work. It was a relief when the book was finally finished, but when I gave it to Joel, my publisher, I found myself echoing Nigel that the book might not be any good.

"I'll be the judge of that," Joel said. So I waited on pins and needles for his opinion. It took him two weeks to get back to me—two weeks filled with anxiety and self-doubt.

"This is one of the best books you've ever written," he finally phoned me to say, and then he added, "I think you've been listening to Nigel."

And so the book was bought. And so the book was published. It went on to achieve lively success. In my years of teaching I have discovered that virtually everyone has an inner "Nigel"—a critic whose sole job seems to be discouragement.

A friend of mine is a Hollywood writer. He sits at his desk for hours daily and grapples with his need for interesting scenes.

"I hate writing," he tells me. "I'm running out of good ideas."

"It sounds like you're being accosted by your inner critic," I venture.

"It's not necessarily a bad thing to have high standards," he retorts, defensive. It is a common block among writers to believe that they should indeed listen to their most critical voice, in the hopes that it will improve their writing. But I have found the opposite to be true.

"Try writing Morning Pages," I urge him. "Let yourself write freely, without straining for perfection."

"I told you I hate writing, and now you ask me to do more writing?" my friend grumbles.

"Yes," I say. "Morning Pages can't be done perfectly. They are strictly stream of consciousness, and they serve to miniaturize your inner critic."

"You really write Morning Pages every day?" my friend asks me.

"Yes," I say, "I've been doing them for years."

"They just sound like work to me," my friend complains. "I'm halfway through a new movie and I'm running out of steam."

"Try the pages," I urge again, but my friend is skeptical.

We got off the phone and I thought over what I had told my friend. In my experience, the critic can't be entirely eliminated, but it can be miniaturized. Miniaturized, the critic seems more like a cartoon character and less like a frightening ogre. Nigel and his like can be shrunk. A mere nuisance instead of a monster, our inner critic can be defeated.

For a little over a month, I undergo radio silence, and then, one day, my friend calls.

"I finished my script," he crows, "and I think I owe you a thank-you. I've been doing Morning Pages daily, and they definitely worked to miniaturize my critic and helped my writing to flow freely."

"You see?" I say. "Writing doesn't have to be a forced march."

"No," says my friend, "in fact, I think I might even enjoy it."

"Just keep at the pages," I coax.

"Surely, if you've done Morning Pages so many years, your critic must be vanquished."

"Not really," I explain. "But I've learned to think of my critic as a cartoon character who is habitually negative without cause. I write, and he critiques. I've learned to write despite his negativity. You, too, can miniaturize your critic. Just keep at the Morning Pages, and allow your critic to squawk."

LOWERING THE BAR

It's 3:00 P.M. on a late summer afternoon. The sky is bright blue with white fluffy clouds that look like sheep grazing. My little dog begs me to walk with her. We set out up the mountain. While Lily is a good sport if my walk is brief, she is happier if I take the time to walk farther. Her ears perk up when we pass a songbird trilling high in the branches of a juniper tree. "Lily, this is fun, isn't it?" I ask her. In response, she tugs at her leash. For her, exercise is a palpable delight. "Okay, Lily," I say, our signal that we've walked far enough. Coming back home, we pause to catch our breath, serenaded by the birds.

Entering the courtyard to our house, I unhitch Lily's leash and let her gambol in the garden. Lily pokes her nose into the mulch below a Chinese maple. She emerges with a mustache on a gleeful snout.

"Time to go in now, Lily," I tell her. Reluctant but obedient, she goes to the front door. I turn the key, crack the door, and hurry inside. Our daily walk is successfully over. Now it is time for another daily ritual: writing.

I settle in my study in my large leather writing chair.

I cue up an album by Cidny Bullens titled *Somewhere Between Heaven and Earth*. The music is expansive, and it moves me to the page. I tell myself I only need to write a little. This is a bribe, a "cheap trick," something I use because it works.

All too often, when we think of writing a project, we think of writing the *whole* project, and we find ourselves daunted. "I'd like to write a screenplay," we think, "but it's so much work, and what if it doesn't sell?" Thinking this way, we talk ourselves out of our creativity. We have set the bar too high. How much better when we lower the bar, when we say, "I'd love to write a screenplay, and I'll bet I can, one page at a time."

I want to talk more about this "cheap trick," one that writers often resist. This is the trick of setting the bar low—"one page at a time"—making the amount of writing that we aim for an easily doable amount. When we set the bar low, we trick ourselves into productivity.

People often say to me, "Julia, you're so productive," and I think to myself, "Anyone can be productive if the bar is low enough." Writing the current book, I aim at a modest goal of two pages daily. I find this amount "perfect"—and encouraging. Writing two pages a day, I write sixty pages a month. By almost anyone's standards, this is speedy. And the trick to such velocity is lowering the bar.

Writing "just a little" yields me a lot. It is, of course, a trick I play upon myself, and a trick I recommend to my students. It is experience that has taught me that "easy does it" doesn't mean "oh, calm down," it means "easy accomplishes it"—"it" being the project at hand. Setting the bar low, at a height well within our reach, gives us a feeling of accomplishment in each day's march. I have tried to write more quickly, only to find I become discouraged and begin missing days.

Setting a goal too high, at four pages, say, rather than

two, I find that I overfish my inner well. When I try to write flat out, I find my writing lacks density. I need to keep my inner well well-stocked, which means, at a moderate pace. I must take one Artist Date weekly to replenish my supply of images. Double the pace, and double the need for Artist Dates. Now I must take two, not one. Taking two requires careful planning, and I soon become discouraged. One Artist Date weekly, and two pages a day—that is the recipe I believe in. On an Artist Date, I may go to a pet store and admire the Himalayan kittens. I may go to a plant store and purchase a bromeliad. Children's bookstores are another favored treat. Each book holds just about as much new information as I can take in. Feeding myself a steady—but gentle—diet of new information fills my well and makes writing easy.

I recently had lunch with a young screenwriter. He was forty pages into a script, and blocked. I discovered in our conversation that he had written the forty pages at a mad dash. Now he was stuck. He had overfished his inner well, writing too fast and failing to take Artist Dates.

"Slow down," I suggested to him. "Try for just a couple pages daily. Don't binge when the writing is going well." I explained that writing slowly would make his project go quickly. He was dubious, but desperate, and so he was willing to give my low-bar approach a try. A screenplay runs a hundred and twenty pages, and so, subtracting the forty he already had, he had eighty pages—or two months' worth of work ahead of him. "I'll try it your way," he said. "After all, this is my first screenplay, and you've written many."

"Call me when you're finished," I told him, and we parted ways. It was two months later that I received his call. He was excited. Working slowly—but steadily—he had finished a draft.

He had a recipe—two pages daily and one Artist Date weekly—which he could apply to all future scripts. "Easy does it" *does* mean "easy accomplishes it." Lowering the bar leads to productivity.

My little dog creeps closer to my chair. She knows not to disturb my writing, but today I have met my quota and I welcome the distraction.

"Come on up, Lily," I say, patting my lap. She jumps up, sweet and affectionate. "We had a good walk today, didn't we?" I ask her. In answer, she grabs for my pen.

PLACE

You have a story to tell. That story is set in a certain place, at a certain time. You, the writer, know this world well. But have you got it on the page? Have you included the details of this world, so that your reader, like you, is able to inhabit it?

Good writing gives us a sense of place. Writing this book, I have included my mountain views. Writing station number three features a large window. That window looks east to the Sangre de Cristo Mountains. From the window to the west, there is a sweep of valley and the Jemez Mountains in the far distance. Close at hand, there is my courtyard and its garden, looming green against the brown adobe wall. I note these details as I write, wanting my readers to experience my home, itself a giant horseshoe.

Writing of Santa Fe, I hope to convey the magic of the city—adobe homes with walled gardens, roses flourishing. The town is built to surround a plaza. At the far east end is St. Francis Basilica, looming tall. When I lived in New York, I wrote of concrete canyons, skyscrapers towering high. Central Park was a verdant carpet flung across the city's midriff. My novel *Mozart's Ghost* detailed an Upper West Side neighborhood. I wrote of delis, pizza stands, and florists. I wrote of diners, one in particular with its cracked vinyl booths. I placed my characters in

A writer, I think, is someone who pays attention to the world.

—SUSAN SONTAG

apartments stacked one atop another. They ventured out on rooftops, catching the sunset over the Hudson.

Leaving New York, I left behind the Chrysler Building with its pineapple-crested height. I traveled west across the flat plains until I reached Santa Fe and its mountains. Tacos replaced pizza. Green chili became a staple. "Christmas"—red chili and green—became a savory treat. Santa Fe woke up my senses. It was a place, and I placed my writing there. But it was more than a mere place. It was luscious, filled with fanciful forms and flavors. Our Lady of Guadalupe stood watch over it all, her blue mantle filled with roses. Here, I write the details of my new home, hoping my readers will feel at home as well.

I live four miles up a mountain from the heart of Santa Fe, its historic plaza. Waking early today, I enjoyed the sunrise with its shades of pink and gold. The snow on the mountain's crest was rosy, and as light spilled down the mountain's flank, my house lit like a lantern. Now it is day's end. The sunset duplicates the sunrise, but my lantern home grows dim, and I flick on the needed lights. I am writing this book room to room as the light shifts. I want to give enough details that a sense of place emerges. Writing does best when it is grounded.

Living in New York, I walked in Central Park. One day I was startled by the sight of a fellow New Yorker with a great yellow python draped around his shoulders. Moving to Santa Fe, I encountered not pythons, but bears. With the swipe of a mighty paw, they tore down my bird feeders, tipped over my trash, left large and ominous tracks on the deck outside my writing room.

"We've got a bear," my neighbor hastened to tell me, and he stayed up late one night to snap a photo of the intruder.

"I have a bear," I told my eastern friends, secretly thrilled.

"A bear!?" they echoed. "Be careful!"

And I did take more care as I slipped from my car to the house. My new backyard is fenced to a height of seven feet. The fence is an effective deterrent to bears. But my little dog, Lily, spots them and sets up a warning racket.

Coyotes slink along the fence line. They, too, disturb Lily, who wants me to know—and to write with a touch of the wild.

Yesterday afternoon I received a phone call from my friend and colleague Natalie Goldberg. "I want to come to see your house," she said. I was delighted. Natalie's life and Natalie's writing are both grounded in a sense of place. She has a garden—in fact, three of them—but the one I envy the most has five fruit trees: apple, peach, apricot, pear, and plum. By contrast, my own new garden is barren, although soon I will do plantings, and then I will watch as new life flourishes.

Before I lived here in Santa Fe, before I lived in New York, I lived in the mountain town of Taos, New Mexico. I had a small ranch—a "ranchito," I called it. It featured multiple views of the mountains surrounding Taos Valley. But of all the different views, my favorite was of two foothills. Natalie described them: "two elephants kissing." As I faced east and south, the elephants made love in my prose. As I faced north and west, the sacred mountain of the Tewa Indians held my attention.

Reading over the books I wrote while living for ten years in New York, I found the lofty Chrysler Building as domineering as Taos Mountain. Writing without a sense of place is writing without moorings. I found place to be central in the great books I enjoyed. Thinking about moving to Santa Fe, I picked up my copy, battered and worn, of Willa Cather's *Death Comes for the Archbishop*. It was filled with southwestern terrain. I loved that book.

Another book, a more modern book, by novelist John Bowers, was titled *End of Story*. It was set in England, in New York, and in Santa Fe. Its heroes—there were several—love to center themselves geographically. As I read Bowers's book, I found myself happily engaged with each of the locales. I so loved the book that as I turned the last page, I found myself flipping back to the story's beginning. I read the book straight through a second time, gasping aloud at the beauty and specificity of the prose.

In film as in books, place is primary. I am friends with a brilliant man, Todd Christiansen, a location scout. He is largely responsible for the "look," the sense of place that his movies entail. Over the weekend, I went to the Santa Fe Film Festival. At the awards ceremony, Todd himself was honored, and I found myself thinking, "Yes, he deserves credit." His job is one that is nearly anonymous, but indispensable nonetheless. Many a director has depended on Todd's expertise. As I write this, the sun sinks in the west as the moon rises in the east. It is a filmmaker's delight. Tonight we are enjoying a three-quarter moon. Its lopsided disk washes the mountain with silvery light.

PROCRASTINATION

It's a bright and sunny day. The sunlight brings with it energy. I'm ready to tackle a difficult topic. Not to be too flippant, but I have put off writing this essay. It's on procrastination, many a writer's fatal flaw. There are so many things to do before writing—change our sheets, vacuum the living room, respond to all our emails, walk the dog. . . . Almost anything can seem more urgent than writing. Like a dog circling its bed before it lies down, we circle our writing before we start. We know we should begin, but beginning seems so daunting. Yet it is starting out that breaks the spell. For procrastination is an evil spell, and as we indulge in it, we become more and more discouraged. Our discouragement is like a deep hole that we keep digging deeper. We need to start, just the littlest bit. A toe in the water leads to a swim.

It takes courage to end procrastination, and we tell ourselves we lack the necessary bravery. But do we? We procrastinate because we think we must write our entire project. But to break procrastination, we need only write our first thought. Our second, third, and fourth thoughts follow. Soon we are writing, and procrastination is a thing of our past.

Take the case of John, a novelist. His first book met with considerable success. His second book found him procrastinating. I suggested to John he try an exercise from *The Artist's Way,* the one that I call Blasting through Blocks. It is one of the most potent tools I have ever created to launch a project into motion, and I use it myself on nearly every creative endeavor I undertake.

"Take to the page," I told him, "and list all of your fears and angers about the new book."

"What good would that do?" John protested. But I insisted that he give it a try, and so he wrote. To his surprise, he had a dozen fears regarding the book, beginning with, "It's a lousy idea." Next, he listed his angers. Once again, he had far more than he would have guessed, beginning with, "I'm angry about the amount of work a novel involves."

"Read me your fears and your angers," I directed John.

"But they seem so foolish," he protested.

"Foolish or not, let's hear them," I said. And so, reluctantly, John read what he called his "laundry list."

"Now start," I told him.

"Just like that?" he asked.

"Just like that!" I exclaimed. "Your procrastination is perfectionism. Just begin."

The scariest moment is always just before you start.

—STEPHEN KING

To John's surprise, he found himself able to begin. His procrastination now seemed like so much nonsense. Blasting through blocks had blown his procrastination to smithereens. It was a powerful tool, and one which he swore he would use in the future. In my many years of teaching, I have seen that although most people feel that their "laundry list" of blocks sounds silly to them, all artists share similar lists of fears, resentments, and angers about beginning. Silly or not, these common blocks are powerful—and I have consistently seen these blocks surrender in the face of this tool.

So remember: procrastination, like perfectionism, always comes down to fear and anger. Blasting through blocks can always clear the way. Like John, face down your skepticism. Your "foolish" fears and angers are boogeymen, nothing more. Be willing to see them dissolve. The simple tool I have been talking about is powerful. What can it hurt to give it a try?

ACCOUNTABILITY

I write daily. After thirty-plus years, I still do Morning Pages. Uphill sometimes, but done nonetheless. I hold myself accountable. I owe myself my stint at the page. Writing Morning Pages is a duty I set for myself. Missing a day or a page, I feel the difference. Pages keep me grounded. I happen to my day, rather than my day happening to me. Pages set my priorities. I stay on course. I'm not swept away by other people's agendas.

I wasn't always accountable. In the days before Morning Pages, I wrote erratically—some today, none tomorrow. Without the rudder of pages, my moods tacked. I was at their mercy. Up or down, I had no control. My projects jerked forward in spurts. I wrote in binges, then suffered from not writing. My temperament swung high to low, matching the day's output. I was often that miserable animal, a non-writing writer. Moody, irritable, and discontent, I was that cliché: the suffering artist. Is it any wonder that I drank, medicating my moods?

Struck sober at age twenty-nine, I was at the mercy of my moods. Without alcohol to buffer them, my moods were savage. I needed a new way to write and to live. I needed to be emotionally sober.

Which is where accountability entered the picture. Living sober one day at a time, I was finding sanity in regularity. I held myself accountable not to drink, and not to indulge in drunken behaviors. My writing remained the one area where I felt out of control. And then it occurred to me: Why not apply the same principles to writing as I did to life?

Easy does it, one day at a time, I began to practice moderation. First things first, I wrote daily. Any day with some writing in it was marked a success. As I wrote more regularly, my moods subsided. An even amount of productivity led to an even temperament. In between movie jobs—enforced writing—I learned to write daily. Washed up in Taos, New Mexico, I hit upon a formula: three pages of longhand morning writing. Regular and repetitive, the pages worked. Done first thing—Morning Pages—they calmed my days and my personality. I became dutiful, accountable. The pages became routine, and necessary. Where once I had depended on alcohol and drugs, I now depended on Morning Pages. I owed them to myself. I've been writing pages three and a half decades now. I hold myself responsible for their daily practice. Writing them, ignoring my inner critic, training it to stand aside, has made all my writing go easier.

"Julia, you're so productive," I'm often chided. I owe my productivity to my daily practice. And for that, I am accountable.

THE DAILINESS OF WRITING

A new day, and a familiar routine: every day at 3:00, my little dog comes to me, asking to go for a walk. She is quite persistent, and leaps happily up when I take her leash from its resting place. We don't walk long—perhaps a half hour—but without her walk, Lily is restless, and having her walk lures her into contentment.

I know how she feels. Lily must walk daily, and I must write. Writing is, for me, a core activity. I experience my life, and I use writing to metabolize that life. Writing becomes a daily habit, a lens through which I filter the world. I have my routine of Morning Pages, and then I have my daily writing on the project at hand. If I do not write, the project, like Lily, yips for my attention. Over the years, I have learned to write when I feel like it and when I don't. Often, the best writing comes on days when I feel stubbornly noncreative.

"Just write, Julia," I coax myself then, and, taking pen to page, I happily obey. As I have said, I am not above praying for help, knowing that prayer—which I sometimes refer to as a "cheap trick"—works.

"Dear God," I pray with confidence, "please give me an idea." Soon enough, the idea comes nudging at my hands, like Lily, eager for her walk.

"You must have so much discipline," people tell me, but I prefer the word "enthusiasm." If my writing is eager to be done, I am eager to cooperate. Like Lily tugging at her leash, my writing sets a pace for me to follow. My pen hurries after my thoughts. I am led forward. Who wouldn't want to write, knowing the good feelings that follow? The part of me that writes is like an eager puppy nudging me for an adventure. I find it best to cooperate, knowing that a day's writing will fill me with happiness.

When I teach, I recommend to my students that they,

too, make of their writing a daily practice. I know that it is far easier to write than not write, and I have listened to many a student who resists this lesson—not writing for one day leading to not writing for two days leading to three and, in time, to a substantial block.

When I was writer-in-residence at Northwestern University, I assigned my students three pages of Morning Pages to be followed by three pages of screenplay—the daily quota. The trick, I told them, was to write daily, but to set the bar very low so their daily quota was easily doable. I used the slogan "Easy Does It," telling my students that it meant "Easy Accomplishes It." And indeed, three pages of screenplay daily yielded ninety pages of script in a month.

I introduced my students to a second slogan, "One Day at a Time," urging them to focus on each day's output, not worrying about the future. Tackled this way, in manageable bites, screenwriting became a pleasant activity.

"Julia, you make it seem so easy," I am sometimes told. This from a screenwriter who is addicted to stop-and-start writing—barren stretches interrupted by binges yielding an erratic output nowhere nearly as steady as my method. "I hate writing," this screenwriter told me, but upon closer questioning, he explained that it was the *way* he wrote that pained and angered him.

"Just try my way," I urged him. "Three pages of Morning Pages followed by three pages of script. One day at a time. Don't overthink it."

Filled with skepticism, he tried my method—and three weeks out, reported a new ease in his output.

"I actually love to write," my once-sour screenwriter told me. "And I finished my screenplay."

"Yes," I told him, pleased. "I knew that you would."

Just as my screenwriter reports his successful writing with glee, I can promise all forms of writing yield to the

The desire to write grows with writing.

—ERASMUS

"easy does it" method. So now, I tell students, if you are working on a project, choose an unreasonably low bar of daily writing and write just that amount, no more. If it takes enthusiasm to write, it equally takes discipline not to over-write, I warn them. The low daily quota yields a quickly increasing piece of work. Writing a small amount daily builds self-worth. After each brief stint at the page, one can feel the flush of accomplishment. An identity as a writer grows a notch more secure. "Easy does it— but do it" becomes the mantra. Do it daily, I urge them, and watch your self-esteem increase. There are few things happier than a writer who is writing.

PORTABLE ART

The daily practice of creativity makes us happy. Painting, sculpting, drawing, acting—these art forms bring us joy. But perhaps no art form is as easily practiced as writing. It is a portable art form. All that is needed is pen and page.

I am writing at writing station number one, my library. I sit in a large leather chair and gaze out the window at the mountains. The view is impressive. The mountains are steep and majestic. Clouds wreathe their peaks. It is raining on the heights. A peal of thunder warns that the storm is coming my way. I pad to writing station three, with its view of the piñon tree—habitat for tiny birds. I watch as they flutter branch to branch. They are engaging, seeking shelter from the coming storm. My phone shrills, and I answer it at writing station number two, my exercise room. The caller is my friend Jacob Nordby, reporting that it is one hundred degrees in Boise. It has been sweltering for two weeks. But rain is promised over the weekend, bringing with it a welcome cool. Balancing the phone on one shoulder, I step onto the treadmill. I walk thirty-five minutes daily. As with Jacob's call, I talk as I walk.

"Are you on the treadmill?" Jacob asks me now. He can hear my steady footfalls. The window here looks out into the branches of a large juniper tree. Ravens enjoy its bows. I enjoy the ravens, boldly peering in my window. I watch their antics with delight.

Writing station number four calls to me now. I perch on a chair in my courtyard, alert to the further rumble of thunder. I sit, enjoying the garden, until the rain starts to spit. I move back indoors, back to writing station number one, the library.

Moving room to room, station to station, I cherish my portable art form. I write longhand, carrying my journal with me, recording my varying views. I sometimes paint, but find myself feeling tethered to the spot I first set up my supplies. How much better, I think, to enjoy the freedom writing affords me. I may stay at one station, or go to all four, if I am restless. If I am very restless, I tuck my journal under my arm and drive down the mountain to town. My favorite restaurant serves as writing station number five. I order grilled salmon and settle in to watch my fellow diners. The restaurant does a brisk business, and I enjoy the varied crowd. At a nearby booth, an elderly couple is sweetly solicitous. A corner table hosts a pair of young lovers feeding each other tasty morsels. A table for two feeds a solo diner like myself. The entree of choice? A delicacy: lobster tacos. My salmon arrives, grilled to perfection. I order flan for dessert. Lingering over the confection, I jot a note. Diane, my favorite server, has lost weight. It becomes her. Signaling for my check, I think the meal was a bargain—delicious food and enjoyable people-watching. My journal records it all.

Driving back up the mountain, I think to myself, "That was a good adventure." Journal in hand, I wasn't lonely. I love my portable art.

TASKS

1. Just Twenty Minutes: Sometimes getting started is the hardest part of writing. This week, set a timer for twenty minutes. Promise yourself that you have to do "just" twenty minutes, and then you can stop. Notice how this works. Does this tool help you to begin? Are you eager to do more than twenty minutes, once you have started?

2. Perfectionism: Perfectionism is a block, not a building block. We often tell ourselves that perfectionism is "having standards," but in fact, it is a stalling device. Fill in the following sentences as quickly as possible, with whatever comes to mind:

   If I didn't have to do it perfectly, I'd . . .
   If I didn't have to do it perfectly, I'd . . .
   If I didn't have to do it perfectly, I'd . . .
   If I didn't have to do it perfectly, I'd . . .
   If I didn't have to do it perfectly, I'd . . .
   If I didn't have to do it perfectly, I'd . . .
   If I didn't have to do it perfectly, I'd . . .
   If I didn't have to do it perfectly, I'd . . .
   If I didn't have to do it perfectly, I'd . . .
   If I didn't have to do it perfectly, I'd . . .

3. Inner Critic: All of us have an inner critic, that voice of doubt who knows our Achilles heel like no other. Fill in the following:
   Name your critic. You may wish to name it after a person—a teacher or relative who doubted you in the past, or a villainous cartoon character—or you may wish to make up a name. (Mine, as I have mentioned, is named Nigel.)

What is the most common thing your critic says to you?

What is the doubt you are most likely to believe from your critic?

What is the worst thing your critic has ever told you?

Take the worst thing your critic has told you, and turn it into a positive. For example, if your critic tells you that you will never be original and have nothing to say, convert this to "I am wholly original and have many things to say. My writing is fresh, interesting, and unique."

4. Blasting through Blocks: This is one of my favorite and most powerful tools. Number from one to twenty and write down every fear, resentment, anger, and worry you have about your project. When you finish, see if you don't have a surprising store of energy and determination to move forward—despite your fears.

5. Place: Establishing place in our writing connects us to our reader, and our reader to us. This is a two-part exercise:

Choose a spot in your house. Sit and write a paragraph describing and establishing the place.

Go out into the world and choose a spot—it could be a park bench, a cafe, a beach—and describe the place. What can you capture of your environment on the page? What are the smells, sounds, and colors you experience? What is the temperature? What is the mood? Write a paragraph describing exactly where you are.

CHECK IN

1. How many days did you do your Morning Pages this week? Are you able to get to them quickly and do them without interruption or distraction?

2. Did you take your Artist Date? What was it? How was it? Did you experience synchronicity, optimism, or a sense of a benevolent higher power? All three?

3. Did you take your walks? Are you able to do them alone and without distraction? Did you try walking out with a question and seeing if you returned home with an answer?

4. Did you hit your daily quota? How many pages are you into your project? Do you feel a sense of excitement as you watch your page count building?

TRUST YOUR PROCESS

By now, you are in motion with your writing—and it is time to lean into trusting your process, your ideas, and yourself. The essays of this week will guide you as you work to write with honesty, while supporting you through the very human issues all writers face at one point or another: jealousy, anxiety, and the credibility attack—as well as synchronicity and glee. You will be led through periods of silence, encouraged to ask for guidance, and emerge into hope.

You are now "in the water," and this week will support you in riding the waves of the process with faith and grace.

TRUSTING YOUR IDEAS

I am friends with a stalled writer. I say "stalled," not blocked, because I have optimism that my friend will write again, just . . . later. He has successfully written three books, and he loves to write. The problem is, he doesn't know what to write. He has ideas—many ideas—but he doesn't trust them. Listening to him over the months that he has been stalled, I have heard him conjure many an idea, then shoot it down.

"That sounds good," I'll say.

"You think so?" Doubt reverberates in his voice.

Another day, another idea. "That sounds good," I'll say again.

"You really think so?" He's not sure. My friend is a

fine writer, and his ideas are fine as well. He could write well on any of them, if only . . . if only he trusted his ideas. The author of a fine book on creative unblocking, he doesn't use his own tools. Instead, he listens to the voice of his inner critic, a voice which whispers on any idea, "It's not good enough."

Good enough for whom? The inner critic is never satisfied. It sidles like a sidewinder, hissing its judgments. My friend, a brilliant man, condemns himself as stupid. Instead of recognizing the perpetual negativity of his critic, he believes each new volley of vitriol. Instead of dismissing his critic's views as cartoonish—"Thank you for sharing"—he takes them to heart.

He could use the affirmation, "I'm a sane and sound thinker." "My ideas are solid and trustworthy," he could affirm further. Affirmative prayer is a potent tool in the warfare of positive versus negative. "I trust my own thinking" can become a worthy weapon. Pledging our loyalty to our own thoughts helps to deflect the critic.

"You'll be excited," my friend phoned to tell me. "I've bought several speckled journals, and I plan to write by hand. You write by hand, and it serves you. I think it might serve me as well."

"I think it might," I reply. My own experience is that writing by hand leads me an idea at a time. If my friend can trust an idea enough to start, handwriting should carry him forward. It certainly does me.

I have one more idea to entice my stalled friend. I voice it despite its simplicity. I tell him, "Take pen in hand. Number from one to ten. Finish this phrase ten times: What I'd really like to write about is . . ."

My friend snorts his skepticism that so simple a trick will actually work. "Now pick one," I continue, unfazed by his resistance.

"Just like that?" he says, incredulous.

You can, you should, and if you're brave enough to start, you will.

—STEPHEN KING

"Just like that," I tell him. "Writing doesn't have to be hard."

"Now that's an idea!" he exclaims. Over the phone line I can practically hear his writing gears click into place.

"So use it," I tell him. I get off the call feeling cautiously optimistic.

HONESTY

Writing requires courage. Not a lot, but enough to say, "I think I'll try to write." Trying to write takes daring. After all, we have a mythology that tells us writers are an elite few. My experience—four decades' worth—tells me something quite different. I have watched many timorous people take pen to page, and with wonderful results. Just yesterday I received a note: "Dear Julia, I am sixty years old and I have just completed my first children's book. Bless you."

It has become my belief that just as all of us can speak, we, too, can all write. All it takes is the willingness to try. As we attempt to enter the writer's world, only one quality is necessary, and that is honesty. If we take to the page with honesty, we will take to the page with success. Honesty requires a desire for our writing to be of service. This posture brings humility, and humility is inviting. The reader responds to our open heart. When I write, I ask myself always, "Am I being honest? Am I being authentic? Am I being of service?" These three questions, answered in the affirmative, yield me a piece of writing that withstands scrutiny. The same will be true for you.

All too often, the novice writer asks the wrong questions—questions like "Am I brilliant? Am I impressive? Am I memorable?" Asking the wrong questions, we find ourselves straining for writing that is the distillate of our ego's demands. It is when we set aside ego, striving instead for honesty, that our writing acquires a natural, unforced authority.

Faced with the question "Who can write?" I find the answer to be "All of us." Writers are not a special few. They are, instead, anyone who puts pen to page with the intention of speaking the truth. It is the desire to share accurately our perceptions that gives a writer voice. When we are willing to be authentic, our words take on the patina of truth. And it is truth which allows the writer to connect to the reader. And truth is a commodity available to us all.

It begins with Morning Pages, where we express—for our eyes only—our heart's truth. As we write pages, we are tutored in honesty. As we strive to write with accuracy, we become increasingly honest. In time, this honesty is carried from our pages into our projects. We write with rigorous honesty, and this wins for us our reader's faith. Born by sharing our vulnerability, we earn the right to write, and our writing "rights" our world. Is it any wonder I love to write?

VULNERABILITY

Tonight is a full moon, but clouds block it from sight. A light rain spits against the windows. It's a good night for staying in, but I am restless. Restless, I phone a friend.

"Julia, my life is so boring," my friend laments—but she is a writer whose life is far from boring. She's written a dozen books, all interesting, all autobiographical.

"Write about it," I urge. "Write about your boring life," I tease her.

In our mythology, writers are tough, steely, invincible. But in reality, writers are anything but. A good writer is a vulnerable writer—one who writes not from invincible strength, but from vulnerability. The best writing comes from the heart, and the heart is tender.

When our writing feels dull or flat, it is because we are refusing to say something we consider unsayable. We are refusing to be vulnerable, to share our secret heart.

Whenever we are willing to be totally honest, our writing has "spice." As we strive to become comfortable with an uncomfortable truth, we become daring. Risking what may feel like—and often is—a large risk, we are being obedient to ourselves. Another friend of mine, an esteemed writer, recently took to the page, convinced that her relationship was boring, and so was her prose. Writing further, striving to tell an untellable truth, she wrote, "I miss sexy sex. We cuddle, but there's no passion." Putting her honest complaint on the page rendered her writing spicy, not dull.

Another writer wrote, "I am uncomfortable with my current weight. My clothes don't fit, and my image of myself no longer feels glamorous. I need to lose twenty pounds."

Still another writer wrote, "I'm afraid that my thinking is hackneyed. I don't dare to say what I really feel."

What all of these writers have in common is a need to be more authentic. As they dare to be honest, their writing catches fire. The conviction that they are boring fades away. All it takes is courage, but courage can be hard to find. The privacy of Morning Pages brings bravery. Honest on the page, we learn to be honest in life.

A beautiful woman in her early sixties exclaimed to me, "Julia, you mean I'm supposed to write how I actually feel? I keep two journals: a public one in which I am spiritually evolved and uplifting, and a private one, which I hope will be destroyed, because in its pages I am often petty and afraid."

"Try to reverse the order of your journals," I advised her. "Dare to let your private journal be more public. After all, what you're confessing there is the human condition. Posing as holy when you feel anything but makes your

Write what disturbs you, what you fear, what you have not been willing to speak about. Be willing to be split open.

—NATALIE GOLDBERG

writing hollow, and that is what you mean when you complain it's dull."

In writing how we really feel, we open ourselves. And when we are open, we are vulnerable. The greatest writing reveals the human condition, and that condition is vulnerable.

Writer A connects with a new and passionate lover, no longer willing to settle for a largely platonic relationship. Writer B takes to the treadmill for long walks that chisel away at her weight. Writer C dares to express new thoughts and insights. Writer D makes public her private thoughts. All of these writers are taking the risk of trusting the universe.

Writing from vulnerability, the writer finds strength. It is a paradox that in tenderness we find power. The human heart, as writing reveals, is a delicate mechanism prone to sentimentality and reverses. The heart is open, admitting to contradictions. The heart does not pose to an inhuman strength; rather, it reveals itself in vulnerability.

ANXIETY

The sky is gray. Not a serene gray, a turbulent gray. Gray on gray, weather pending. A storm is on the march, pushing down from the mountains, 13,000 feet, to here, 7,800 feet. I am anxious, waiting for the storm to hit. Anxious, I turn to the page.

Anxiety is energy: banked energy. For writing, this energy is a useful fuel. Anxiety feels like fear, and, like fear, it is a spur that prompts us to write. And so we begin. "I am anxious because . . ." But anxiety resists easy naming. We can, and often do, feel anxious for no apparent reason. Unlike fear, which is specific, anxiety is vague, free-floating. And so we say, "I'm anxious and I don't know why." That admission is the first foothold on the path back to normalcy. We surrender to our anxiety, better to give in than to fight, which only heightens anxiety. After all, anxiety is a mood, and moods are time-limited and fleeting.

Now the rain pelts down, but it makes a louder than normal *ping*. Of course it does, for the rain is now hail, and the hail roars as it lands. Now my anxiety has something to latch onto. Hail the size of marbles mixes with hail the size of billiard balls. Will a window shatter? I'm anxious, and my little dog is anxious too. She rushes from room to room, seeking a quiet refuge, but there is none.

"Lily, it's okay, we're safe," I tell her and myself. As abruptly as it started, the hail stops. An unearthly quiet seizes my senses. I am braced for the hail to begin again, but it does not. Slowly, tentatively, my anxiety starts to subside. Was it really carried by the weather?

I set pen to page, detailing the storm. I write rapidly, trying to outrun my anxiety. A word at a time, a drop at a time, my mood grows gentler. My writing slows. I catch myself missing the velocity of my anxiety. I tell myself that creatively, anxiety is my friend: an uncomfortable friend, but a friend nonetheless. I resolve that the next time anxiety hits, I will go straight to the page, using the fuel it provides me.

It is not long before I have my chance. The next morning, wind whips through the piñon tree. It rattles my windows and draws things to scale. Nature is mightier than I. My daughter, Domenica, in Illinois, snapped photos of fallen tree limbs. She called me to say they were on a tornado watch. "What are the odds of a tornado hitting them," I wondered, frightened. Seeing the photos, I saw that the tornado had indeed come close.

Here in New Mexico, the wind is not a tornado, but it is mighty. It sends storm clouds tumbling down from the mountains. Little Lily, weather-sensitive, hides beneath my desk. She wants to be near me. I want to be near her as well. We each take creature comfort in the other's presence.

I take pen to page, turning to an old trick: rhyming away my anxiety.

> *Is this the norm, this mighty storm?*
> *Hail, rain, and wind—when will it end?*

I find that rhyming gives me a sense of safety.

> *Lily, dear, please come near.*
> *Little lassie, so cute and sassy.*
> *Lie down, Lily, at my feet.*
> *You are ever very sweet.*

And Lily does lie down at my feet. She is, ever, very sweet. I smile at her obedience to my little rhymes. I catch myself thinking of my friend and fellow poet Julianna McCarthy. Just yesterday, Julianna laid out for me her formula for happiness: gratitude and humor. If, today, I am short on gratitude, I am long on humor.

> *What's this? I dare. I think it's a bear!*
> *No, it's the wind. I think it's my friend.*
> *It will stop blowing. It could be snowing.*
> *I'm snug and warm. It's just a storm.*
> *My silly little rhymes make me smile.*
> *At least, I think, I still have style.*

And so I pad to the kitchen, where I will heat a casserole. My little dog pads after me. When I eat my casserole, she will munch her dog food. "Monkey see, monkey do." When I set my pen down, she grabs for it. Yes, she is a writer's dog, I joke. Her antics make me laugh. If only she could really write, she might say the same for me:

> *This little poem goes out to my owner.*
> *Without her, I would be a loner.*

She gives me treats, and water and food,
And although it seems quite rude,
She makes me wear a silly collar.
And although I am no scholar,
I read her needs for fun and laughter.
I deliver what she's after.
Owner, dear, have no fear.
Your little Lily hovers near.

And Lily does hover near. The wind has set our electronic alarm system off. It makes a loud beep, and Lily is frightened by the sound. I'm frightened too. I call Nick, who lives twenty minutes away.

"I'll be there in twenty," Nick says. I reread my rhymes as I wait, laughing to myself lightly. The rhyming has calmed my anxiety yet again. True to his word, Nick knocks at my door twenty minutes later. He called the alarm company and was told it wasn't the alarm that was going off, but a smoke detector. Climbing on a ladder, he reached the smoke detector, only to realize that the beep was coming from the carbon monoxide detector. He disabled it, and the beeping stopped. Climbing off the ladder, he was met by a grateful Lily. She, like me, felt rescued. Perhaps a rhyme of gratitude will be in order next.

TRY RHYMING

I was walking north, up the dirt road near my house. It was a tranquil day, and a tranquil walk, until, a scant footfall ahead, I nearly stepped on a snake. It was dead, run over by a car, but no matter. It was still a snake, and I am terrified of snakes. I sprang backwards, giving the dead snake a wide berth. What if it wasn't dead? I retreated all the way back to my house. I crossed the courtyard looking for more snakes. A lizard darted near my foot, but I wasn't afraid of lizards—just snakes. This snake was silver, the color of death. I hurried into the house, where I grabbed a pen and paper.

I wrote:

Oh silver snake, you make me quake
I feel such fear, a viper near.

The little couplet siphoned off some of my fear. After all, if I could write about the snake, I had some power over it. Writing of what I feared, I feared it less. This became a lesson for me.

Not everyone fears snakes, but everyone fears something. For my friend Bob, it is bears. He summers high in the Sangre de Cristo Mountains—bear country. At night, he arms himself with a heavy-duty flashlight, shining a wide arc on his path. He rushes from his car to his cabin, dreading a bear looming near. By day he finds bear tracks, so his fear is fueled. It's not just his imagination: there are bears. Hearing his fear, I take pen to page for him.

Oh mighty bear, you make me dare.
I shine a light, its beam is bright.
I find my path, avoid your wrath.
I hurry home, I'm not alone.

Like the snake poem, the bear poem vanquishes fear. Writing is powerful, more powerful than our fears. A mountain lion has been spotted near a neighbor's house. It lurks atop an adobe wall, ready to spring down on its prey. I borrow a cue from my friend Bob: I carry a powerful flashlight, shining its beam into the darkness. I spot no cat. Safe at home, I write:

A mountain lion, I am wary.
A mountain lion, the thought is scary.

To be an artist means never to avert one's eyes.

—AKIRA KUROSAWA

A giant cat with teeth and claws
Its appetite makes me pause.

Writing out the little ditty, I find myself relaxing. I am safe indoors. Let the big cat prowl the perimeter. I will come to no harm. And so I say, write of what you fear. And so I write.

If you're clever, you will never
Ever need to fear again.

The next time anxiety strikes, try a little rhyming—and see if it doesn't help it to subside.

JEALOUSY

Jealousy is a map. It tells us—with excruciating precision—just where and for what we yearn. Make no mistake: jealousy is a tough-love friend. It lets us know in no uncertain terms the territory and accolades we covet. And we feel so petty! Jealousy tightens the chest, digs for a grip in our stomach, sets a toe tapping in anxiety. We don't like to feel jealous, although we have been assured jealousy is a normal human emotion. "Maybe your jealousy," I think, "not mine." My jealousy is my smutty little secret.

I hate to admit—even to myself—that I am jealous. At its root, jealousy is a stingy emotion, grounded in fear—fear that there is not enough good to go around.

But there is enough good, although jealousy tells us otherwise. Fearful at its core, this emotion diminishes our self-esteem. We will *never* attain the object of our desire, jealousy tells us. And "jealousy" is a dire word. "If 'it' hasn't happened yet, it will never happen," jealousy asserts. Instead of provoking us to increased action, jealousy tempts us to despair. Instead of urging acceptance of

God's delay, we take it to be God's denial. Someone else has won the prize, and our envy dictates our position—lower—on the totem pole of life. Jealousy causes us to lose perspective. Instead of seeing our many wins, we focus on our losses. We perceive ourselves in black-and-white terms. Compared to the illustrious "someone else," we are a loser.

Jealousy wears blinders. Instead of taking in the broad sweep of life, it focuses narrowly. Instead of seeing that we have triumphs—often many—we see only our defeat. "And it will always be this way," we scold ourselves. But will it?

Jealousy can be turned to our advantage. After all, it points us in a direction we desire. At its best, jealousy is a goad. It asks us to try harder, rather than admit defeat. Trying harder, we may win through after all. No longer jealous of another's achievements, we hail them now as a colleague, even inspiration.

A woman friend of mine offers yet another perspective. "My jealousy," she tells me, "involves a man, not work. In retrospect, I'm grateful I didn't get who I thought I wanted."

And so it is possible—difficult, but possible—to see God's wisdom in our thwarted desires. Our jealousy may be an opportunity for spiritual growth. In point of fact, it always is, for jealousy requires of us honesty. We must admit our dreams and desires. We must admit our anger at being passed over. Jealousy brings with it the gift of self-knowledge. All things considered, can it be all bad? Painful, yes, but as sages have remarked, pain is the touchstone of spiritual growth. Jealousy asks us to grow.

HUMILITY

Due to our persistent mythology, many of us are convinced that writing is hard. This is because we want to write perfectly. We want to write brilliantly, cleverly. We want to write so that no rewrites will be necessary. We want our writing to impress people. We want it to prove how smart we are. In short, we ask it to do everything except what it is intended to do, and that is communicate. When we are willing to write from a spirit of service, our writing becomes more clear, more persuasive, more honest. Most of us want to take pride in our writing, when what is called for is humility.

Bernice prided herself on her clever writing. She built sentence upon sentence showing off her brilliance. Imagine her distress when I suggested to her that she was too clever, too brilliant, that her writing put people off rather than inviting people in.

"But Julia," she wailed, "I work hard at my writing. I'm proud of it."

"That's just the problem," I told her. "Your pride gets in the way of your communicating. I'd like you to try an experiment. Try writing from a spirit of service. Try letting a higher power write through you. Just give it a try," I urged. My own experience had taught me that her trying would work.

Reluctantly, angrily, Bernice did as I suggested. To her surprise, the writing improved. It became less about being clever and more about being clear.

"Why, Julia, this is so much easier," Bernice confessed.

"That's because you're no longer asking your writing to do two things—both to communicate and to impress." Ironically, Bernice's new writing was impressive.

When we write from a spirit of service, our writing communicates clearly. When we write out of pride and ego, trying to be smart, our writing becomes more shallow and manipulative. Is it any wonder our readers are repelled? When we have the humility to focus on "getting something down," instead of "making something up," our writing becomes user-friendly. It becomes close to conversation. We listen, and we write down what we "hear."

I never exactly made a book. It's rather like taking dictation. I was given things to say.

—C. S. LEWIS

We begin to have the experience of our writing "writing through us." Like Bernice, we become a channel—or, if you would, a conduit—through which writing flows freely. As we practice the art of listening, we do become more open, more able to receive that which wants to be written. As we listen, our writing becomes sure-footed.

Writing benefits from clarity, and clarity comes from humility. Stripped of ego, our writing becomes accessible, heartfelt. However, writing from the heart instead of from the head may take all the humility we can muster. For often, ego refuses to budge. Novice writers often strive to be "smart," and yet there is such a thing as being "too smart" to write well.

Good writing is clear writing, and clarity involves simplicity. When we try to be "smart," our writing often takes on needless complexity, causing the reader to puzzle over our precise intentions. Good writing is user-friendly. Simplicity makes our intentions clear, so that the reader knows precisely what we are talking about. When we write simply, we write well.

It is ironic that we often flagellate ourselves as "too dumb" when in reality, the opposite is true. We are too smart—intellectual poseurs—who embellish our ideas with unnecessary frippery—as I have just done! Ego-driven, we may wish to pose on the page, showing off our brilliance and erudition. Such posing, however, is actually a bar to communication. We are "too smart" for our own good.

The clearly spoken facts are far more persuasive. When we write simply, we write well.

PATIENCE

The day is gloomy, rain pending. The mountains are blurred. I put pen to page, wishing I could write faster, wishing the rain would hurry up and come. I am impatient. I've been writing this book for what seems like a long time. The pages mount up slowly but steadily. I follow my own advice and set the bar low. "Easy does it," I remind my impatient heart. "Easy accomplishes it. Slow down." And so I do.

I have learned through my long years of writing that patience is a necessary virtue for a writer. I have learned that going slow serves me better than going fast. As a young writer I rushed ahead, overfishing my inner well. My writing suffered. It was fast, but it was also thin and strained. Rewrites, often extensive rewrites, were necessary. My hurry didn't serve me.

What a relief it was when I slowed down. Writing by hand was slower than writing by computer, but the quality of my writing improved. No longer thin and strained, my first drafts became succulent. Taking a cue from famed editor Arthur Kretchmer—"put it in, put it all in"—I began to include details that I had been too rushed to include before. Rewrites, while still necessary, became lighter. There simply wasn't as much to "fix."

Writing by hand became a habit. I found one word led to the next. My trickle of words became a steady flow, fluid and forceful. Rather than rush ahead, I lingered, savoring the details. Writing went from being a race against time to being a walk, with each footfall, each word counting. As the years piled up and the books piled up, I became patient. Experience taught me that patience served. I tutored my impatient heart to calm down, and found my slow and steady pace paid off. Editors remarked favorably on the "polish" of my work. I moved smoothly, project to project, no longer exhausted by a sprint to the finish.

Now, I could wish to go faster, but discipline tells me to go slow. On this book I am averaging three longhand pages a day. At the halfway mark, I pause to congratulate myself on the progress I've made. Slowly and steadily I have put to the page what I know about writing.

A word after a word after a word is power.

—MARGARET ATWOOD

A word at a time, a thought at a time, writing is the distillate of our experience. The nectar of our psyche, writing deserves not to be rushed. Writing Morning Pages daily, we learn to transcribe each thought as it comes to us. Writing on our projects, we find ourselves moving ahead a thought at a time. We are learning patience, waiting for each idea to arise. Our writing becomes quite literally thought-full. Our prose becomes richer. Patience is the key to fine writing. I love to write, and patience has taught me to savor the process.

DISCIPLINE

My Morning Pages track the weather. I wake to a sky that spills icy rain onto the mountain's flank. Lily begs to go out for her walk, but it is too wet for our usual adventure. I turn up the heat to fight the chill. The furnace gives off a low, dull roar. I set to the page.

"If I had the discipline, then I'd be a writer," I am often told. This thinking, one more time, has its roots in our mythology about writing. We believe that writing is difficult and that "discipline" is necessary to pull it off. We are encountering here, one more time, perfectionism—the belief that what we must produce is a polished product. But what if we loosen the reins a little bit, and talk about having a writing *practice*? What if writing is something best approached more casually, as a daily rendezvous, a meeting with a lover, that we embrace with enthusiasm? If writing is a daily practice, something done for love, then the idea of discipline falls away. We look forward to our clandestine coupling, not as a chore, rather, a delight.

"Julia," says Carl, "I used to think writing was difficult, something best approached sternly, but now you tell me writing can be done more easily, approached with joy as much as rigor?"

Yes, I do believe writing is a joyful process. On any given day, we can choose to write Morning Pages. This choice brings with it feelings of self-esteem and satisfaction. Yes, we are happier when we write. Is it any wonder I love to write?

"Put it on the page," we tell ourselves, and when we do, we experience delight. Although our mythology speaks of discipline, our experience speaks of pleasure. Writing is naughty. There is something close to glee in setting our thoughts to paper. Enthusiasm, after all, is lighthearted, while discipline is harsh. This is, one more time, where Morning Pages enter the picture. We write our pages upon awakening, and the pages themselves awaken us further. Writing Morning Pages makes us smart. When it is time for us to turn to our "real writing," we do so with energy. Our ideas flow freely; we are nimble on the page. Writing, after all, is a demonstration of faith in ourselves and our ideas.

"Julia, you make writing sound so simple," my students sometimes complain.

It *is* simple. From our Morning Pages, we have learned that we can write from whatever mood we find ourselves in. We learn that we can make art when we don't feel like it. There is a simple question we can ask ourselves. That question is, "Am I being honest?" Honesty brings artfulness. There is a fluidity to our thoughts when we simply let ourselves write from honesty. We put pen to page and set down our ideas as they come to us. We do not struggle. We do not fret. We do not worry. We trust our first thought. We rejoice that our thinking is clear.

Lily sits by my chair, staring at me as if to ask, pointedly, "Can we go *now*?" She retrieves her leash. Taken with her enthusiasm, I promise her a short walk followed by a toweling off and a nap by the fire. As with writing, it is joy, not discipline, that brings us out into the weather, into action.

Amateurs sit and wait for inspiration, the rest of us just get up and go to work.

—STEPHEN KING

THE CREDIBILITY ATTACK

The mountain's flank is dappled by the shadows of passing clouds. One minute it is light; the next minute it is dark. It makes me think, once again, of the way our mood shadows what we write, causing us to believe first that it is terrible, second that it is great. It takes practice to disbelieve the verdict being cast. Just at the moment, a massive thunderhead looms overhead. It darkens the entire mountain. A dark memory comes to mind.

When I was a young writer, I was a columnist for the *Los Angeles Herald Examiner*. It was a prestigious gig, and one which I thoroughly enjoyed—except for just one thing. Every time I went to the paper to turn in a column, I was seized by an encounter with what I call the Credibility Attack. I feared being turned away from the paper because I was "too young" to be a real writer, much less a columnist. On a rational level, I knew my fears were groundless. All I had to do was show my ID and then turn in the column of the day. My fears were groundless, but very real. On the drive from West Hollywood to downtown Los Angeles, I would rehearse a defensive speech, ready to deliver it upon arrival. Of course, it was never needed.

In my years since my days as a columnist, I have learned that the credibility attack is a cunning enemy. I have written many books, but each book brings a new attack from Nigel. As I turn in my pages to my editor, I "hear," "It's just not good enough. Who will want to read it?" It does no good to remind my psyche of my previous successes. The credibility attack is not logical. Instead it goes for my creative jugular, declaring always the utter worthlessness of my worth and my work.

I am not alone in suffering credibility attacks. My friend and colleague Sonia Choquette is also beset by this monster. She has written a dozen books. She has a large and enthusiastic following. And yet, each time she finishes a manuscript, she undergoes a bout of despair and depression. I am among her early readers, and her pages come to me with her worried proviso, "I don't think it's very good." But her books *are* good. She has simply bought into the credibility attack.

Another writer and friend suffers mightily from this syndrome. Each time she finishes a book, she falls into despair. She makes submissions waiting for the axe to fall. Each reader becomes an executioner: "Off with her head." But the axe does not fall. Her writing is good, and, as she says to me, "If only I could trust my talent." When each book is accepted by a publisher, she waits for reviews, convinced by the credibility attack that they will be bad. Logic and a dozen past successes tell her to trust, but she cannot. But no. Her prose holds up.

The credibility attack defies logic—and history. It is not only illogical, it is vicious—a true monster. I say "monster" knowing that it sounds dramatic. But the credibility attack is dramatic, and standing up to its assault requires courage. "My writing *is* good," we must insist to ourselves.

The thunderhead moves to the mountain peak and then beyond. Bright light touches the mountain's flank, reminding me, when the credibility attack darkens my day, that "This too shall pass."

ASKING FOR GUIDANCE

A half-moon lights the nighttime sky. I walked Lily late, just as dusk was falling, and her white coat glowed phosphorescent in the twilight. Safely back at home, she stretched out on the love seat, determined to keep me company. She has an angelic temperament, at once merry and empathetic. Tonight she senses my lonely mood and does her best to offset it. As I put pen to page, she nuzzles me, encouraging a flow of words. I want to write about Higher Forces, those energies which write through me. I write "LJ," for "Little Julie," and ask my question:

LJ: Can I have guidance, Higher Forces?

Then I listen. I hear:

"Little one, you are on track. There is no error in your path. You are led carefully and well." That is by way of greeting. Next I ask: "Who are you?" And I hear: "Little one, we are happy to remain anonymous."

"Are you angels?" I ask further, pushy.

"Little one, it little matters what you call us. Know that we are, as you sense, gentle, powerful beings who intend you great good."

And so, respecting their desire for privacy, I address these benevolent beings simply as "Higher Forces." So addressed, they answer me promptly. I am, to them, "little one," a term of endearment. Their wisdom is calm yet specific. They directly address the topics I raise. When I tell them I am reluctant to directly approach the Great Creator, they sympathize. They tell me that they too feel awe when addressing the divine. To them, my reticence is understandable. They feel a shade of it themselves.

I ask these Higher Forces for guidance daily. Most often, I ask them for help with my writing.

"LJ: Can I have guidance about my writing?"

They respond, "Little one, do not worry that you are out of ideas. We give you words and thoughts." And so they do. I am led, as they have promised, "carefully and well."

Writing into the void, following their guidance, I write a word at a time, a thought at a time. What comes next is none of my business, just what comes now. "There is no cause for anxiety," I am tutored, and so I try to simply trust. I ask, as now, "What more do I need to say?"

The answer comes swiftly: "Tell people we are reliable. Ask them to experiment with our lead."

And so I must report that the Higher Forces have

proven themselves to me to be reliable. I myself have experimented with their lead and found it to be trustworthy. They have dictated a path that was safe to follow. They have told me, "Do not doubt our goodness," and they have said, in summary, "All is well."

SILENCE

A harsh wind whips down from the mountains. My piñon tree lashes side to side. I sit curled on my love seat. It's twilight and the dimming light makes the wind seem even more sinister. Little Lily has already taken herself to bed. The elements affect her. I sit, pen in hand, writing for guidance. I hear, "You will be led," but nothing further. My chimney rattles, shaken by the wind. I feel rattled myself, wishing for more specific guidance.

When my phone rings it is a welcome distraction from the weather. The caller is my friend Ed Towle, sequestered in Santa Monica.

"How's the writing going?" he asks me.

"Don't ask."

"That well?"

"I've no idea what to write tonight."

"So your guidance is a blank slate?"

"Exactly."

"Write about that. You've been going along receiving abundant inspiration and suddenly it dries up. What do you do? Is it like having the internet go down? If so, can you leave it alone and come back later?"

Ed chuckles at his own analogy. Inspiration *is* like the internet. You tap into it and you receive information from a mysterious source. Like the internet, it is a miracle of higher communication, always available until—suddenly—it is not.

Before Ed called, all good cheer, I was brooding. Writing for help, I heard, "You will be led." Such optimism seemed too good to be true. And so I asked again, "What should I write?" Silence greeted my plea. And then Ed called suggesting that I write about my blank slate and so now I am doing that. Reporting an experience of radio silence—an experience perhaps common to my readers. An experience Ed has had.

The moon, past full but still luminous, washes the mountains dark silver. I pray to the maker of the moon, asking for some hint of direction. I lecture myself: "Sometimes silence is golden. Relax."

And so I try to relax, trusting that like the internet, mysteriously blinked off, inspiration will blink back on, its lapse done with.

I try not to panic, but the "blank slate" causes anxiety. I am accustomed to having inspiration function like guardrails, keeping me to a straight and narrow path. With its guidance, I feel secure, happily going forward, guided and guarded. It may sound "woo-woo," but it works for me.

Writing is an act of faith, not a trick of grammar.

—E. B. WHITE

The wind is quieting down. The chimney no longer rattles. The phone rings again. This time it is my daughter, Domenica. I tell her I'm enduring radio silence and she says to me, "It's like a spiritual quest. Sometimes you have to have faith in the absence of proof." She pauses, then adds, "On a spiritual path, there are always these windows of silence. Jesus, Buddha—they all had them. The message is sometimes silence is okay." Domenica is both thoughtful and rueful. She continues.

"I never liked what I think of as Los Angeles spirituality in which the seeker claims, 'I'm *always* guided.' That seems to me to be artificial, prideful, not accurate. In my experience, inspiration comes and goes—and the going is a normal part of the spiritual path."

I appreciate my daughter's thoughts. I feel her remarks calming me down. So it is normal to miss guidance sometimes—normal and to be expected.

Taking this advice to heart, I still cannot resist asking for inspiration one more time. "Can I please have direction?" I ask the ethers. Blessedly, I hear a message back. "Little one, all is well." That is all, but it is enough. I put away my pen and paper. I will write again tomorrow.

CHANGING GENRES

It's another dark day, storm clouds hovering. It's monsoon season in Santa Fe, and showers sweep in daily, in midafternoon. Little Lily grows restless as the rains approach. Like me, she prefers a sunny day. No such luck today, and so I flick on the lights. Now I can see to write, and write, I will. The topic of the day: changing genres.

A glance at my bibliography shows I have written in many genres—crime novel to romantic comedy, prayer books to plays, short story collections to self-help guides. I've written for love, skipping genre to genre, giving little thought to the alleged danger of changing forms. As a rule, I've written on spec, completing books without a contract, selling all but two. I have not played it safe, sticking to one form, trying to guarantee a success. Instead I have followed my muse, writing what wants to be written. This has kept writing fresh for me. Each book has had its own trajectory.

"Julia, you're so bold," I am sometimes chided. But following my muse has not felt bold. Rather, I have felt obedient, writing along the trail the muse has laid out, following inspiration where it leads. Such obedience brings with it happiness. I think, "Yes! I'd love to try that," and then I do. A dutiful season of too much teaching was shattered by the crime novel *The Dark Room*. My muse was being naughty, dark instead of light. A change of tempo and of mood, dodging the bullet of St. Julia, not wanting to be typecast. I felt glee. From the crime novel, I turned next to romantic comedy. My muse was tired of darkness and needed some laughter. *Mozart's Ghost* provided plenty. I loved writing it, often laughing aloud about my characters' antics.

From novels, I turned to plays, and from plays to teaching books. Each genre scratched a different itch. *The New York Times* dubbed me "The Queen of Change." I accepted the mantle gladly, posting on my website, juliacameronlive.com, work in multiple genres, playwriting to poetry, musicals to music. I know there are those who would caution against changing genres, feeling better safe than sorry. But my experience tells me that writing stays fresh when you follow the muse and not the market.

HANDWRITING

It's nightfall. Darkness is descending. A crescent moon peers over the mountains. I move my hand across the page. Thoughts follow thoughts. That is the magic of writing by hand: each stroke of the pen moves me forward. I'm writing this book by hand, essay after essay. My book *The Listening Path* was written by hand, as was my book *Seeking Wisdom*. I am comfortable handwriting, and I hope that ease shows on the page.

The moon tonight is a sly crescent. It is the moon of new beginnings. I begin this essay speaking of the moon, hoping, like the moon, this essay will wax full. I want this essay to be particularly persuasive. I believe firmly in writing by hand, and I want that belief to be contagious. Yes, I know, writing is faster by computer, but I don't think fast is what we're after. What all of us seek is depth and authenticity. We want to transcribe our thoughts exactly. Writing by hand makes that possible. Let us say the issue is how we feel about X. Typing, we might say, "I feel okay about that." Writing by hand, we have time to query, "What do I mean by 'okay'?" We may discover we feel fine—or not so fine. "Okay" is vague, and our actual feelings are particular. Pen to page, we grow specific. We dare to write precisely what we feel. Handwriting keeps pace with our thoughts. We are not rushing ahead, nor do we linger behind. There is a momentum to the hand. We write what's next, and the hand often tells us. Our projects unfurl themselves. Pen in hand, we are in touch with our higher selves, that intuitive spark that guides us. We are led carefully and well. There is no error in our path.

Morning Pages train us to follow our train of thought. Morning Pages trace our unspooling consciousness. We follow thought to thought, and discover that is a portable skill. Morning Pages prepare us to work on our projects. We become nimble, moving adroitly thought to thought. We listen with an inner ear that guides us. We write what's next without second-guessing ourselves. We don't take mental cigarette breaks. Many of us find that by slowing down, we actually speed up. Our handwritten pages mount up.

There is a cohesion to drafts written by hand. Clarity of thought is an often unexpected dividend. It is as though, writing by hand, we cannot lie. Whereas on the computer, we could whiz past an evasion, writing by hand, we are led to greater honesty. Heightened awareness of ourself as author leads to more truthful writing. This honesty connects us to our readers. They can sense the authenticity of our work. Our vulnerability is inviting.

Manhattan-based psychiatrist Jeannette Aycock swears by handwriting for a greater accuracy in her notes about her clients. "I've been practicing psychiatry thirty-six years now, and all of them handwritten. Writing by hand, I put in details that typing, I might skim past." Aycock puts a hand to her heart. "Writing by hand, I put in how a patient looks, what mood colored our session. Writing by hand, I get to know my patients better. I know them this high—then this much more." She gestures high, and then higher still, with her hands. "I take a lot of notes," she explains. "I wouldn't dream of using the computer. It's too detached."

Seeking to connect rather than detach, we find hand-writing as therapeutic for us as for the good doctor. Like her, we discover that our writing becomes more specific. As now, I record the slimmest crescent moon, silver in an inky black night.

SYNCHRONICITY

"If you write Morning Pages, you will experience syn-chronicity," I tell my students. "You will find yourself in the right time, in the right place, meeting up with fortu-itous circumstances that appear to be more than mere co-incidence. Synchronicity is the uncanny meshing of our inner and outer worlds."

How do I know what I think until I see what I say?

—E. M. FORSTER

We write, "I think I should get a dog for companion-ship," and the very next day, we are told of a stray that needs a good home. We write, "I wish I spoke a foreign language." A notice on the bulletin board at church an-nounces classes in beginning Italian, the very language we most thought we'd like to learn.

Writing Morning Pages, we notify the universe of our dreams, wishes, and desires. The universe, in turn, sets about the business of fulfilling those desires. It is as though we have placed a carryout order, and need only pick it up.

As we write, we open ourselves to Higher Forces. We receive hunches and intuitions that lead us down our proper path. At first, we may mistrust such spiritual in-put. But as we continue to write, our intuition gradually becomes a working part of the mind.

Sometimes this guidance feels off-kilter as we strive to make logical sense of the input we are receiving. Our rational mind longs for logical input. But logic is not the be-all and end-all. Rather, we must learn to follow guidance that, at first flush, makes no rational sense. At first, we may struggle with resistance. Accustomed to trusting logic, we find it difficult to abandon the rational in favor of the intuitive. However, as we pursue a path of daily writing, our hunches become increasingly insistent. As we act on those hunches, we become surefooted on the spiritual path.

Michael wrote in his Morning Pages that he yearned to make films. "But I'm too old and it's too late," he scolded himself. But this was not the case. In his weekend newspaper, he spotted an advertisement for an adult beginner's filmmaking class. He was delighted to know its price was well within his budget. He phoned the number listed and secured a slot. The teacher assured him he was not too old to learn filmmaking techniques.

"I can't believe it," Michael told me. "I no sooner got clear on my desire than my desire was fulfilled."

Many times a student will tell me that synchronicity came into play in seemingly impossible circumstances. Carla yearned to write a book on her experience as a nurse practitioner. It would be quite inspirational, she felt, if only she weren't afraid to try writing. She got clear on her desire, and realized that what she wanted was a coach. Her very next case sent her to caring for a retired editor who was looking for something meaningful to do in retirement. The editor thought Carla's idea for a book was worthy of her time and attention. Here was a case of synchronicity involving two people's dreams. Carla wanted to write a book, and the editor wanted a project.

The intuitive part of our mind is directly connected to our higher self. The input we receive is often a shortcut to our dreams and goals. As we open ourselves to this higher guidance, we are tutored in faith. Gradually, we come to trust the voice of our intuition as it speaks to us. The "funny feeling," the inkling, the hunch, all guide us on our path. We are led carefully and well. There is no error in our promptings.

"Julia," I am sometimes scolded, "synchronicity feels like luck."

Synchronicity *is* luck, I answer. But it is luck that you make yourself through writing. I urge my students to try writing with specificity about their desires. I urge them to be alert for their "luck." Many a creative dream is well within our grasp once we accept the notion that the universe is a benevolent, helping force ready to fulfill our wishes. Often, all it takes to experience synchronicity is the setting aside of skepticism. As we learn to expect synchronicity, we find we can experience it in myriad ways, large and small.

At forty years of age, Alan dreamed of going to Harvard for a master's degree. His dream met with acceptance, once he took the action of applying. His heartfelt letter of application met with the desire of an acceptance committee's recent mandate to open the gates of their prestigious institution to older students.

"My Morning Pages urged me to apply. I set aside my skepticism and wrote to the university of my dreams. To my great surprise, they took my letter to heart and offered me a slot. I was ecstatic, and I found that my gratitude for the opportunity gave me tenacity in my studies."

Stories like Alan's come to me often. I have come to believe that synchronicity can be counted on.

WRITING TO METABOLIZE LIFE

I begin my day with a welcome call from my friend Judy Collins. "I'm on the road and I'm writing," she carols. "I'm grateful." Judy is eighty-two, with the energy and drive of someone far younger. She gives concerts nearly every other day, jetting crisscross across America and Europe. Her voice is as clear and pure as one of the Rocky

Mountain streams of her childhood. She writes as often as she sings—eleven books to date, using writing as a spiritual path.

Writing is a way to metabolize life. Intense emotions benefit from writing, although at first it may seem the opposite. We say goodbye to a lover whom we will not see again for many months. Our emotions are deep and heartfelt. Putting pen to the page, we find ourselves sorting through our feelings. On the one hand, we are glad for the great adventure our lover undertakes. On the other hand, we already are missing our beloved companion. Contradictory emotions swirl through our consciousness. At first, we feel loss, a poignant welling up of all that is dear and known. But what's this? Next, we are feeling anger. How dare our lover leave us alone and abandoned? Now we are angry at ourselves. We feel clingy, needy, bereft.

The true alchemists do not change lead into gold; they change the world into words.

—WILLIAM H. GASS

"I should never have cared in the first place," we scold ourselves, and then, in contrast, we feel, "It's good that I have loved, and there will be other loves." What began as a welter of confusing ideas resolves itself into the single feeling: regret. The kiss goodbye was poignant. The backwards glance was poignant, too. Writing the details of parting, we find ourselves deeply connected, not only to our lover, but to ourselves.

We have a mythology which tells us that writers write from pain, and it is true that painful feelings can nudge us to the page. But writers write from joy as well as sorrow. Love letters are a case in point. "My darling," we write, "how I love you. You bring me great joy. Just knowing that you exist and that we are connected causes me to feel happiness. You are in my heart. I cannot express adequately the delight I feel in your companionship. I will write you daily while you are gone. A letter back from you feels like springtime. The day is balmy. All of my sentiments are glad."

Writing from joy, we find ourselves waxing lyrical. We

use pet names and endearments. We reach for language to accurately express what is in our heart.

The birth of a grandchild is cause for jubilation, relief that the long labor is safely over and wonder at the miracle of birth. Tiny fingers and tiny toes, a Cupid's bow mouth, dimples, knees—all these details come alive for perpetuity on the page. Yes, writing is spacious enough for great joy. Momentous occasions yield to the page. All manner of feelings can be traced by writing. All that is required is the willingness to report accurately to the page.

Judy is a case in point. Her latest book, *Cravings,* details her decades-long battle with food addiction and bulimia. Blessed by a shining and angelic public persona, she privately fought the demons she details in her book. A woman of great courage, she lays bare her struggles, scouting a path for others to follow. She has survived great hardships—the death by suicide of her only child, a son—a tragedy which she has turned to good use in helping others similarly afflicted. Forty years sober, she often speaks on her alcohol addiction, once again helping others to find their path. A multifaceted artist, she was recently nominated for a Grammy for her songwriting. Although she didn't win, she thoroughly enjoyed the attention her nomination brought to her. Famous for decades, she is graceful in her fame, wearing her celebrity lightly.

Judy is open about the heartache and tragedy in her life, but she is also filled with gratitude for each day's march. Through all of it, she writes—books, music, lyrics. When I lived in New York, we had dinner most Monday nights, and would share stories of life and writing. Today I am in New Mexico, where I spot a lone doe picking her way gingerly through the chamisa. Her grace and beauty remind me of Judy.

Write what you know.

—MARK TWAIN

HOPE

It's sunset, and the clouds wreathing the mountains are apricot, reflecting the setting sun. It rained an hour ago, and the colorful sky is a remnant of the storm. Where lightning flashed, the newly serene sky holds the promise of a calm and peaceful evening, the hope of a rosy dawn and clear day tomorrow. I say "hope" because weather is uncertain, and hope holds optimism. As a writer, I am trained to hope—hoping this book will turn out well, hoping it will be bought and published. Hope, for a writer, is a necessary companion. We write for love, not money, although we all hope for a goodly sale.

Writing requires hope. Notwithstanding our track record, we hope each word is well-chosen. We hope our sentences hang together. We hope our paragraphs persuade. Hoping for the best, we do our best, hoping that it is enough. Optimism, hope's younger sister, tells us that it is.

Optimism and hope travel together. We have an experience of both as we write. We hope our writing will serve. Optimistically, we believe that it will. Writing is an estimable act, after all. It is good to write, and we hope, always, to write better. When we are writing, we have a sense of the rightness of the world. Our will, and God's will, are aligned. We are co-creators with our creator. Is it any wonder writing feels so good?

As I write, the apricot fades from the sky. Twilight settles in—lilac, gray, and then black. Over the mountains, a new moon is rising. It is the moon of auspicious beginnings. I hope for its blessing. Writing this essay, I'm filled with hope. Pen to page, I feel joy. Joy, like optimism, is hope's younger sibling. When I have hope, I have a joyful heart.

Faced with this world's difficulties, it takes courage to have a joyful heart, to elect optimism—hope—over despair. To write takes courage, daring to sound a hopeful note in the face of cynicism. Writers practice bravery. Hoping always for a better world, they bring it into existence a syllable at a time. With their words, writers span continents. Their hope is to be understood. Their mantra is "I understand."

FAITH

I believe writing is a spiritual path. When we put pen to page, we come into contact with higher realms. Call this contact the muse—or simply inspiration—it is a flier into the divine. Like all spiritual paths, writing leads us forward. We write from where we are, and we are led ahead carefully and well. We experience hunches, inklings, inspirations. Moving out on faith, we put them on the page.

Writing requires faith, a firm grounding in the worthiness of what we have to share. Faith requires courage. We *dare* to write our thoughts. Putting pen to page is an assertive act. We stand naked before the reader. We clothe our thoughts in words, each chosen with care. We have faith in what we are saying. It is an act of faith that we are able to write at all. We have faith, too, in our readers. We trust that they will comprehend what we are driving at. Putting words on a page, we have confidence that we will be understood.

Isn't that what a poem is? A lantern glowing in the dark.

—ELIZABETH ACEVEDO

Faith is something that we exercise, and something that we increase through writing. Faith is a gamble on optimism. We have faith, and hope that we are right. As Churchill remarked, "I am an optimist. It does not seem too much use being anything else."

Writing requires optimism, and it breeds optimism. Pen to page, we are bold. Faith fills the coffers of our hearts. If we try to write without faith, we soon build despair. We feel the contradiction of our experience. Writing all but demands faith and optimism. Goaded by our dis-comfort, we soon move to correct our course, writing one more time with a faithful heart.

When we write with faith, our very personalities expand. We find ourselves writing with joy, and joy is the touchstone of the spiritual path. Our faith is user-friendly. Our faith is generous. Faith-filled writing issues to the reader a joyous invitation: "Come in. Let me share my thoughts." And so, as we have dared to be intimate, the reader dares as well. Our worlds build a bridge of con-nection. Our faith illuminates a path. Our readers follow where we lead, feeling, "Hosannah."

TASKS

1. Asking for Guidance: Take pen to page and write out a question. You may wish to refer to yourself as I do: "LJ" for "Little Julie." Listen for a response. Do you find that you hear wisdom back? Your ques-tion can be about anything: your writing project, a relationship, or just generally, "What do I need to know?" Remember, the response may often be suc-cinct or feel overly simple. But there is wisdom in simplicity. How does what you "hear" back make you feel? Can you make asking for guidance a reg-ular habit?

2. Jealousy: All writers experience jealousy. Writing quickly, make a list of everyone you are jealous of. Next to their name, write what you are jealous of. For example: "Paula: she has published her songs." Now, write a small action you could take. "I could write a song of my own." Jealousy may be pain-ful, but there is always potential action contained within it.

3. Trusting Our Ideas: Take pen in hand. Number from one to ten and quickly fill in the following:

What I'd really like to write about is . . .
What I'd really like to write about is . . .
What I'd really like to write about is . . .
What I'd really like to write about is . . .
What I'd really like to write about is . . .
What I'd really like to write about is . . .
What I'd really like to write about is . . .
What I'd really like to write about is . . .
What I'd really like to write about is . . .
What I'd really like to write about is . . .

Now, set a timer for five minutes. Choose one topic from your list, and write about it for five minutes.

4. Synchronicity: Take pen in hand and list five examples of synchronicity since you have begun this course. Synchronicity appears in surprising places, and increases as we work with the tools of this book. Looking over your list, do you see that you are partnered by a higher, benevolent Something as you go through this process?

5. Writing to Metabolize Life: Number from one to five, and list five emotionally charged topics or moments from your life. They may be joyful, tragic, confusing . . . what matters is that the emotion is a strong one—good or bad. Now, take the most charged topic from your list, and write about it for fifteen minutes. When you are done, do you sense a new perspective on the topic?

CHECK IN

1. How many days did you do your Morning Pages this week? Are you able to get to them quickly and do them without interruption or distraction?

2. Did you take your Artist Date? What was it? How was it? Did you experience synchronicity, optimism, or a sense of a benevolent higher power? All three?

3. Did you take your walks? Are you able to do them alone and without distraction? Did you try walking out with a question and seeing if you returned home with an answer?

4. Did you hit your daily quota? How many pages are you into your project? Do you feel a sense of excitement as you watch your page count building?

RESIST YOUR
RESISTANCE

All writers encounter resistance at different points along the journey. The trick is to resist your own resistance. At this point in the process, you have accumulated many pages. This is to be celebrated! At the midpoint of the course, it is natural to experience doubt, fear, or anger. This week will move you through the issues that you resist from within—as well as the resistance that meets you from the outside in the form of toxic friends and crazy-makers.

It is possible to resist your resistance, and to continue forward in the way that matters the most: making progress on your writing project.

MOOD

I woke early, filled with energy. I found myself eager to write and so I set my pen to the page. I want to write about treachery, the treachery of mood in writing. Yesterday, I spoke to my friend Julianna McCarthy, an actress and poet. We agreed that mood colored our perceptions of the work at hand.

"It's so treacherous," Julianna exclaimed.

"Exactly the word," I agreed.

Both Julianna and I have been writers for a long time, and we know enough not to wait for the "right" mood to write. A positive mood is a luxury, not a necessity. Long years of practice have taught us that good writing can happen on a bad day. A more unpleasant lesson taught

*I don't wait for moods. You
accomplish nothing if you
do that. Your mind must
know it has got to get down
to work.*

—PEARL S. BUCK

us that bad writing could happen on a good day. The trick, as I said to Julianna, is to write no matter what. She agreed, and told me that she would put in a day at the page. Later, she would evaluate.

"Later" is the time when we go back over our writing, not in the heat of creation, but in the cool light of assessment. I have learned, through practice, that mood cannot be trusted. A dark mood darkens my perceptions of my writing. A light mood brightens my perceptions. And so, I try to be dispassionate, setting my mood aside, good or bad, and aiming for neutrality.

I recently wrote a play. In the fever of creation, it seemed perfect. But reading it in the cooler "later," I saw that it could be tightened and improved. And so, I set to work to fix it, leaning into what I consider to be the "craft" of writing. I have learned to set my mood aside and stop insisting that my work is perfect. Instead, I tell myself, "It's not perfect, but it is good—and good can be improved." So setting my mood to "neutral," I set to work.

Take my play: I found what it needed was a simple reshuffling. A scene that I had placed late in act 2 instead belonged early in act 1. The change tightened the play and improved it. The cool reassessment of craft was what was called for.

"Ah, yes," Julianna sighed when I told her the saga of my fixes. She agreed both that the fixes were often necessary, and that the craft of doing them was even enjoyable. Mood, treacherous mood, was to be ignored.

While I consistently tell myself that any writing is good, long years at my craft have taught me that "good" writing and "bad" writing are very close together. On any given day, my prose is simply "Julia's prose." My ticks— and tricks—are near automatic. Take yesterday. My mood was cranky; ideas came slow and stubborn. No, I didn't feel like writing, but I did write. I practiced what

I preach. The sky yesterday was cold and blue, with tiny white clouds floating like saucers. On my walk with Lily, a raven cut the air, sounding its raucous *caw, caw, caw.* Its voice was rough-edged. My voice felt rough-edged as well. But I kept writing. I did not allow my sour mood to spoil a day's work. After all, moods pass, and writing remains.

U-TURNS

My phone rang early this morning, rousing me from a happy dream about horses. The caller was an East Coast friend who had forgotten the difference in our time zones.

"Julia, I'm stuck," my friend complained. "I have two weeks until my novel is due to my editor. I can't write the climax. What should I do?"

"Just finish it," I told him.

"I've tried," he replied. "I just can't."

"I don't have a magic wand," I said, "but I do have a bag full of tricks. Take an extra Artist Date. Put yourself into a week of media deprivation. Do the exercise Blasting through Blocks."

"But Julia," my friend protested, "it's not that easy."

I sympathized. "The spell of U-turns is very strong. Undoing a U-turn takes courage. Picking up the thread you have dropped takes self-worth. My tools help to build it."

Let us examine a typical U-turn. A writer is working productively until something happens, and that something can be good or bad. Let us say the writer shows the fledgling work to a creative monster who savages it. Discouraged, the writer does a U-turn, and stops writing.

Or, alternatively, let us say the writer shows the fledgling work to a person who raves about its brilliance. Intimidated, the writer does a U-turn and stops writing. U-turns, grounded in fear, are common to all careers, and sneaky.

They are powerfully negative. Sometimes the writer abandons a single piece of work. Sometimes the writer abandons the art form entirely.

In 1974, I wrote a short story which I showed to my best girlfriend, a fellow writer.

"Oh, Julia," she scolded, "if you publish this you'll ruin your career."

At the time I had no career, but that didn't keep me from taking the scolding to heart. I buried the short story in a drawer and focused my writing abilities on journalistic profiles. There, my short story skills served me in good stead. But from 1974 to 1994, I never wrote another short story.

And then, during an Artist's Way course, I suddenly recalled my abandoned story. I had done a U-Turn, I realized, and I told my group the details of my discouragement.

A scant two weeks later, driving with my father across Texas, I heard a voice. It said, "Karen's new life began ten miles west of the Pecos River."

"Dad," I announced, "you drive. I think it's a short story." And so, while my father piloted us across the panhandle, I listened to the voice in my head and wrote my first short story in twenty years.

Once back home in Taos, New Mexico, the voice continued with a second story and then a third. Undoing my U-turn, I wrote a dozen short stories. They became my collection *Popcorn: Hollywood Stories*. I published them with glee. By undoing my U-turn, I gained a whole book. Such was the propulsion of my unblocked creativity.

U-turns are powerful and cunning. Often, the writer fails to realize that a U-turn is at hand. Like my friend the novelist, he mysteriously loses interest in the story he is telling. Or he skips over from one art form to another, as I did from short stories to profiles. I did not realize I had done a U-turn. I simply thought my journalism career had gotten hot. My writing met with approval. I basked in the attention it brought. My new art form was seductive. It caused me to have amnesia about the old.

Many of us have multiple U-turns, thwarting our talents in many arenas. Doing this exercise, we may at first have amnesia. I had forgotten my short story U-turn. Recalling it gave me the power to write stories again.

Take pen in hand. Moving an art form at a time, record your U-turns. Did you ever do a U-turn in writing? In visual arts? In dance or movement? A category at a time, recall your U-turns. Share your U-turns with a trusted friend. Can you take a small step to undoing it? Even the smallest step will give you back your power.

Make no mistake: U-turns are powerful, but the undoing of them is even more powerful.

ANGER

It's a dark and stormy day. The sky mimics my topic: it is angry.

Anger is energy. Energy is fuel. Many of us fear our anger. We think anger is bad. We think anger is destructive. We do not see anger for what it is: a tough-love friend. Anger tells us when we have been betrayed, by others or ourselves. We have crossed a boundary, and anger is the result. Feeling anger, we are able to tap an inner resource. We find words come rushing to the fore. Anger is a goad provoking us to self-expression.

Writing is an act of self-cherishing. As we check in daily with ourselves, we give voice to our many hidden dreams and agendas. As we ask ourselves, "How do I really feel?" we answer with increased authenticity. Rather than being vague—"I feel okay about that," we are specific, daring to put on the page our true feelings. If we are hurt, we say so.

When we welcome our anger, we become articulate.

We are able to say what we mean and mean what we say. Our words may come in a rush. Anger whips us forward. We find ourselves dashing our sentiments onto the page. We may barely find time to express our thoughts.

"Why, I'm furious," we may exclaim, caught by surprise, startled by the intensity of our feelings. Anger pushes us past our censor. It allows us to say the unsayable. "I'm furious" becomes the tip of the iceberg. Words spill on the page as we articulate, "I'm furious that . . ." When we express our anger, we express our true feelings. Uncensored, we tell it like it is. "It makes me furious that . . . ," we say, and we experience a rush of adrenaline. We are daring to tell the truth. As we write out our authentic feelings, we experience a flow of words which spell out precisely the transgression we are experiencing. "I hate it that . . . ," we write, and as we do, we feel the reality of our emotions. We are moved to action. Yes, anger is energy. Yes, anger is fuel.

"I hated the way Jim talked to me in the meeting yesterday," Alice wrote. "He took credit for my idea." In the very next meeting, cued by her anger, Alice spoke up. "I'm glad you liked my idea, Jim," she said, taking ownership of her own idea. "I was angry," she confided to me, "and my anger gave me a map. It pointed out just where I felt betrayed. I was able to speak up for myself. Later on, I felt proud."

The pen is mightier than the sword!

—EDWARD BULWER-LYTTON

As we write, we become known to ourselves, and increased tenderness to the self we are discovering is the reward. As we dare to bare our souls—anger and all—we find ourselves lovable. Increased tenderness is the result. Our daily pages tutor us in self-knowledge.

Writing daily, we stay current with ourselves. There is no error in our path. As we write our wishes, dreams, and hopes, we embrace ourselves. We honor our impulses to our aspirations with kindliness. Our gentle attention yields increased productivity as our creativity is channeled along fruitful lines. We embrace the guidance we receive through our anger. As we do so, we are led further and further into active self-love.

FEAR

Pen in hand, you are ready to write. That is, you are *almost* ready to write. You have a moment or two of procrastination to get through. You see, you are afraid. Let us say your first sentence comes to you. With it, comes the thought, "Is that good enough?" You judge your sentence harshly, as you are afraid of its being judged. Perfectionism is at hand. You want your sentence to be perfect, by which you mean brilliant.

You want to write freely, but fear marches alongside your train of thought. Your second sentence brings to mind, "Is it good enough?" You screw your courage to the sticking post. You begin. And as you do, the miraculous happens. Your fear subsides. You are committed now to what you are writing. Judgment be damned. Your thoughts are flowing—that is, they are if you have accepted sentence number one.

This is where discipline enters the picture. Discipline tells you you must accept your first sentence. You must believe in the validity of your first thought. It is indeed good enough. In point of fact, it may be very good indeed.

Our first thoughts are often precisely the right thought with which to begin. They are often bold. They are often assertive. They hold open a gate for further thoughts to follow. They do all this if we embrace them, if we set aside our fear of being judged. Our fear, after all, is as damning as we let it be. We're afraid of being judged—what? Stupid, naive, gullible. A nasty litany springs to mind. In all likelihood, we are not those things, reason tells us. At least not all of them. Our fear of judgment verges on paranoia. After all, more good than bad can come from putting pen to page. Believing this, we move past our fear of judgment.

"But what if I look foolish?" The scary thought rears its head. Looking foolish is something to be avoided, but perhaps the way to avoid it is through affirmative action. As we boldly embrace our thoughts, we issue a dare: disagree with me or discount me at your own risk. By daring to write, we are persuasive. We disarm our critics by virtue of our daring. Fear tells us we will be judged. Reason tells us we will survive, that our most damning critics risk appearing foolish.

Fear is an obstacle on our road. As we dismantle our fear, what is the worst that can happen? We move on to the page. A sentence at a time, we make our case. Rather than appear foolish, we soon appear wise. Daring to put pen to page, thought to thought, we march past our fear into courage. Fear itself is the bullet which we dodge. Writing is the weapon which wins the day. Our daring to write, to trust our first and further thoughts, casts fear as a boogeyman, a bully that we stand up to. The only fear we have to fear is fear itself.

RISK

Most of us have an idea of just how creative we are. We think we know our talents and their limitations. We know what jumps we will try, and we will risk so far, and no further. The risks we will take are small, and don't move us out of our comfort zone . . . And then we encounter Morning Pages. The pages train us to take risks. They dare us to move outside our comfort zone. The daily risk of writing how we really feel trains us to expand.

"I didn't know I felt that way!" accompanies a fresh realization. Our self-knowledge deepens as we risk becoming more honest. This risk encourages further risks as the pages nudge us forward.

"You might want to try . . . ," the pages venture, naming a proposed risk.

"I can't do that," we exclaim, dismissing the risk that would move us beyond our comfort zone.

"Are you sure you can't?" the pages may whisper next, and again meet with our resistance. The risk which loomed large looks smaller somehow. And so we say, tentatively, "I don't think I can." But doubt has crept in, as the pages are persistent.

"I think you could," the pages persist. And, fed up with their nagging, we finally exclaim, "Oh, alright, I'll try it." And, trying it, we risk risking.

Make no mistake: pages are a tough-love friend. They challenge us to change our size, to become larger, more daring. Tutored by them, we alter our perceptions. We see that we are far more creative than we previously thought.

"You will be writing radiant songs," my pages persisted . . . and persisted. I dismissed their optimistic guidance as grandiosity, until, exasperated, I did as was suggested. I now write music regularly. Three musicals and two children's albums are the fruit of my risking a risk.

My colleague Emma Lively listened to her pages and went from being an unhappy violist to a happy composer. "Composing was my childhood dream, but I had given up on it. I thought it was beyond my reach, but I was wrong. Pages dared me to try, and so I dared." Her musical, *Bliss,* debuted to standing ovations.

Daniel Region, actor-director-voiceover talent, listened to his pages as they urged him to try writing fiction. To date, he has finished two short story collections and a novel. "When the pages broached the writing risk, I went from 'Hell no' to 'Why the hell not?'" Daniel discovered he loved writing, and writing loved him.

The worst enemy to creativity is self-doubt.

—SYLVIA PLATH

I used to teach in Chicago, in a room with a low Styrofoam ceiling. Imagine my delight when a student tapped the ceiling with a broomstick and revealed ten more feet of space up to an old-fashioned pressed tin ceiling. We are like that room, with an artificially low ceiling on our talents. Morning Pages are the broomstick that reveals our true height.

KEEP THE DRAMA ON THE PAGE

It is a dramatic day. Wind whips through the piñon tree. Little birds take shelter in its innermost branches. I sit in my living room, calm despite the turbulent weather. After all, drama belongs on the page. We have a mythology which tells us writers' lives are dramatic, but this mythology does not serve us. Writers' lives are best nondramatic. It serves us to keep drama at bay. And so I write tonight. My words bring me both calm and clarity.

I have learned through hard knocks that indulging in extreme emotions leeches my writing of power. We have only so much emotional energy, and when we expend it foolishly, our work suffers. I am close friends with two other writers—writers who are indulging in a bitter fight. "Be on my side," both writers have entreated me. But what serves their emotional needs doesn't serve my creative needs.

"I'm sure the two of you can work things out," I have said to both parties. Such neutrality meets with emotional blackmail as each friend claims that if I were truly a friend, I would take sides. I resist the temptation. I have found through experience that indulging in drama robs me of creative resources. Before I knew better, I had allowed myself to be swept up in the dramas of my friends, and I paid the price. A novel that had been going very well suddenly dried up. I found myself devoid of good ideas, empty of inspiration. My daily writing time—a two-hour chunk in the afternoons—suddenly became my phone time as I listened to one friend and then another about their grievances.

"Pull yourself back from the drama," I advised one of the combatants when she called me for advice. I explained that indulging in histrionics kept me from worthwhile theatrics on the page. She could learn my lesson.

"People will think I'm a nasty person," she complained to me. "They'll think I'm cold if I detach."

"Which matters more?" I asked her. "Your writing, or your self-image as a mensch?"

"When you put it that way, it seems obvious," she responded. "My writing matters more, and besides, if I'm not writing well, I do become a nasty person." And so, reluctantly, my friend extracted herself from her friend's altercation. As her life calmed down, her writing picked up. She made a resolution that henceforward she would keep drama on the page.

Drama can be external or internal, and for the writer, both types are equally damaging. Self-generated drama may show itself as worry or generalized anxiety. But I have found that it is always better to put pen to page than to indulge.

I have a close friend, a writer, who has been suffering from a severe depression. For months she has been plagued by the blues. She blamed it on COVID, but when the pandemic lifted, she had only herself to blame.

"I envy you so," she tells me. "For you, writing is a core activity."

"It can be for you too," I urged her. "Write about anything and everything. Describe your life, including your depression. I think you will find the depression lifts if you write."

"But Julia," my friend protested—dramatically, I might add—"I'm too depressed to write. I can't write. I have nothing to say."

"Nonsense," I told her. "Depression is the perfect goad to get you on the page." For weeks, even months, I urged my friend to stop procrastinating and start writing. "It's just fear," I told her. "Rootless fear that you will have nothing to say."

"Don't sugarcoat it," my friend protested. "And what if it's true that I have nothing to say?" She sighed dramatically.

"Just begin," I coaxed her. "Start with 'I have nothing to say.' 'My heart is an empty well.'" I all but begged my friend to take pen to page. When she is writing, she is merry, and a good companion. Not writing, she is as depressing as she is depressed. "You do have something to say," I told her, "even if all you're saying is 'I have nothing to say.'"

"You're lucky," she scolded me. "Writing is easy for you. I'm just not in the mood." She sounded petulant, like a rebellious child.

"Writing is easy for me because I have learned to write instead of indulging in the drama or waiting for the right mood. You can do the same."

I could feel her resistance. Her drama wouldn't budge. In my Morning Pages, I found myself writing about my friend's not writing. Her writer's block had become a block in our friendship. I had grown tired of hearing her excuses for avoiding the page. Perhaps she had grown tired of her excuses too, because she phoned me one day, palpably happy.

"I'm writing," she announced with jubilation. "I realized I had been operating on the assumption that my Morning Pages had to make sense. That they had to be 'good' writing. But just trying to write feels wonderful."

I did not tell my friend how her writer's block had jeopardized our friendship. Now that she was writing again, she was back to being my cherished friend: lively and filled with ideas.

"I'll talk to you tomorrow," she promised me merrily. "Right now I'm going to write." I looked forward to her call, knowing that as we wrote, all things were right between us.

STEADINESS

The sky is overcast, raindrops pending. The weather is mischievous: clear half the day, stormy the rest. Lily is restless. She hides beneath my desk.

"It's okay, girl," I tell her, but she is dubious. Who can blame her? The rain yesterday turned to hail. Slamming down from the heavens, it made a racket. Lily shook at the noise. Then, as abruptly as it started, the hail stopped. Mere raindrops beat a steady tattoo against the windows. Five minutes of that, and then the storm moved past. The freshly washed courtyard glistened. Lily went to a window and peered out. Coast clear, but for how long?

Back to today, storm pending. "Write now," I tell myself, taking advantage of the relative calm. I have learned to grab time when I can. And so, "It's okay, girl," I tell Lily again. This time she creeps out from under the desk, she, too, taking advantage of the calm.

Nick is due here in fifteen minutes. Lily will beg him for a walk, and he will cast a glance heavenwards, assessing how long the pause is before the storm. A native New Mexican, he has an uncanny ability to predict to the minute when the overcast sky will hold, and when it will drop rain. Caught in yesterday's hailstorm, he reported ruefully that he had left the hail behind him when he piloted his car up the mountain to my house. Today, lest hail come again, he has brought a tarp to protect his car from dents. And what about he himself, I wonder? I marvel at Nick's derring-do.

When he arrives, he tells me of his morning's doings. He hiked a mountain, and now he writes a poem detailing his climb. "I thought it deserved a poem," he says. Like me, Nick habitually puts his experience into words. Rugged yet kind, he greets Lily with evident affection. For her part, Lily is ecstatic at his attention.

"Shall I take the girl for a little jaunt?" he asks. She is tap-dancing as he snaps on her leash. "She really missed yesterday's walk," he says fondly. They head out the door.

My phone shrills. The caller is my friend Robert Stivers, the extraordinary fine art photographer. He confirms the time we are meeting for dinner. We haven't seen each other since pre-COVID, a year and change. We both warn each other that we may look a little the worse for wear.

Back from his jaunt with Lily, Nick and I set to work. We are crafting writerly emails, and we work until it's time for me to go meet Robert. Our rendezvous is set for six forty-five at a favored haunt: the Santa Fe Bar & Grill. I arrive first, and when Robert arrives, I am so glad to see him that I don't spot any telltale fatigue. A handsome man, Robert resembles Robert Redford, wearing his age—seventy—gracefully. We take a comfortable booth and set about the business of compliments.

"You look good, really good, not gaunt," he tells me. I take in his handsome visage. Glancing at our menus, we make short work of ordering. Then we settle in to shoptalk.

Robert is a working artist, a hardworking artist. Most nights find him toiling in his darkroom, "making things of beauty." Like me, Robert works daily, following his muse where she leads him. "I like what I'm doing right now," he says modestly. "I think I'm growing." Robert's growth takes his photographs in new and unexpected directions. "I'm doing a lot of abstract work," he tells me, "and people seem to be responding."

People respond by cash on the barrelhead. Robert makes a living off of his work, and a good living, although he pours his money into more work. "I found an empty warehouse space that I'm thinking of taking—blank white walls. I think they could be good for my work."

"Yes," I say. "You sound excited."

"Do I?" he asks. "I'd need to get a good table and a ladder." Robert grins. "I guess I have a work ethic," he says. Like me, he believes in steadiness. "I just do the work. It's like your pages. You don't plan them, you just show up."

DEADLINES

Deadline: the very term is sinister. Dead . . . line. You will suffer a fate worse than death if you miss it.

"A deadline holds you accountable," says Emma Lively, who is in favor of deadlines as a goad to productivity.

"Deadlines are a nightmare. You want to get the writing done, but done right," says Nick Kapustinsky, who toiled for some years as a journalist with perfectionism as his additional challenge. "Do it on time, but do it perfectly," he recalls his thinking.

"Deadlines assure you will finish in a timely fashion," Emma Lively elaborates. She has a book due with no deadline, and she finds herself dawdling.

"The pressure of deadlines, what a nightmare," Nick Kapustinsky remembers. He writes daily now, but without a deadline looming over him. No longer a journalist, he now finds writing a pleasure, no longer bedeviled by the twin demons, punctuality and perfectionism.

"Deadlines are my friend," Emma Lively sums up her experience. Working as an editor, she divides the number of pages by the number of days she has remaining. This gives her a daily quota. Meeting her daily quota, she automatically meets her deadline.

Deadlines can be imposed by others, or set by ourselves. It is important that in either case they are reasonable, and an "impossible deadline" may be exactly that. And so we must learn to speak up for ourselves, perhaps naming a more reasonable deadline. Think in terms of pressure: too tight a deadline may freeze us up. If, like Emma Lively, you enjoy the pressure of a deadline, count yourself lucky. If, like Nick Kapustinsky, you feel tormented by it, speak up. You may do best setting your own timeline.

How do you set your own timeline? You rehearse the process Emma Lively follows. First, you set your daily quota, remembering to set the bar low enough to be easily doable. Next, you count the number of days it will take you to finish your project. Divide the days by your quota. Finally, go to your calendar, and mark the date you can reasonably expect to be done. This book will run two hundred pages. My daily quota is two pages. I'm now on page 140. That leaves me with sixty pages, or thirty days, to go. It's now mid-September. I can expect to be done by mid-October. That is what I mean by a reasonable deadline.

That word "reasonable" is important. In order to be useful, a deadline must be reasonable. Too rushed or too loose, a deadline loses effectiveness. Use your common sense, and the strategies I've outlined, to test your deadline. Tackle your daily quota, and aim to finish on time. Your deadline may not be deadly.

COMPETITION

So long as you write what you wish to write, that is all that matters; and whether it matters for ages or only for hours, nobody can say.

—VIRGINIA WOOLF

Tonight is a new moon, the moon of beginnings. I tell myself it's auspicious, that the sly crescent of moon brings luck. I have been reading other writers on writing— Natalie Goldberg, Stephen King. I enjoy their thoughts, but I tell myself my own thoughts are worthy too.

Often when we write, we discourage ourselves at the very start by telling ourselves that others have written before, and better. Instead of reaching within and striving to articulate accurately what we think and feel, we look outside of ourselves. Haven't others written better? And they are already published. This is the spirit of competition. Rather than striving to be authentic, true to ourselves, we strive to be "better," better than others. Instead of answering the question, "Am I saying what I truly mean?" we tell ourselves, "Hasn't it been said before, and better?" Reading other writers, we are daunted. We often conclude that their writing is superior to our own. Striving for perfection, we compare our rough drafts to their polished products. Rather than allowing ourselves to write freely, laying track, we censor what we write. Instead of being encouraged by our peers, we tell ourselves that those who have gone before us are stronger and more accurate in what they say.

The spirit of competition kills art. Instead of trusting that what we say will have value, dispirited, we tell ourselves that our work is worthless. After all, "so and so" has covered the same territory, "and better." Our insistence that our work "beat out the competition" actually causes us to create work that is derivative—our worst fear. Looking at the work of others, we say to ourselves, "It can't be improved upon"—but then we try. And in trying, we copycat those we admire. Rather than ask ourselves, "Does my own work ring true?" we credit others with the spark of originality that we ourselves could find if we turned our attention inward.

When we strive to describe accurately what we ourselves think and feel, we find ourselves drawing from an inner reservoir. We "hook" our ideas. They are like beautiful koi swimming just below the surface. As we pull each insight from this reservoir, we connect it to the thought before and the thought that follows. Moving our pen across the page, we explore each thought. We discover our impulses can be trusted. We map our own psyche, and our map is unique and individual. Our work may echo another writer, but, like an echo, it will carry its own voice.

I recently found a book, *Becoming a Writer* by Dorothea Brande. Published in 1934, it advocates both morning writing and creative adventures. In 1992, I published *The Artist's Way,* advocating what I called Morning Pages and Artist Dates. I didn't know about the earlier book, and when I found it in 2021, I found myself feeling not competition, but camaraderie. After all, Brande and I both spoke the truth of what we knew of creativity. Our ideas were similar, but our voices differed, each speaking to the audience of its age.

Reading other writers, I can choose between a spirit of competition and a spirit of camaraderie. Seeing similarities in our thoughts, I can choose to feel validated, not outdone. I can compare rather than compete, finding value in shared thoughts. I am the origin of my work, and that fact alone stamps it as original.

CRAZYMAKERS

This essay may be difficult and annoying to read. It concerns what I call "crazymakers," personalities that are themselves difficult and annoying. Crazymakers create turbulence and chaos. Deadly for the creatives in their midst, enormously destructive, they may be charismatic, frequently charming, highly inventive, and powerfully persuasive. They turn those talents toward creating storm centers, disrupting the lives of those they deal with. Crazymakers thrive on drama, casting themselves as the stars, with everyone else as supportive players, picking up their cues from the crazymaker's crazy whims.

If you are involved with a crazymaker, you probably know it. If you have doubts, read on. Crazymakers break deals and destroy schedules. Crazymakers expect special treatment. Crazymakers discount your reality. Crazymakers spend your time and money. Crazymakers triangulate those they deal with. Crazymakers are expert blamers.

They create dramas, but seldom where they belong. Crazymakers hate schedules, except their own. Crazymakers hate order. Chaos serves their purposes. Crazymakers deny that they are crazymakers.

If crazymakers are that destructive, what are we doing involved with them? The brief but brutal answer is that we are that crazy ourselves. Blocked, we are willing to go to almost any length to stay blocked. As abusive and threatening as life with a crazymaker is, it is far less threatening than a creative life of our own.

If you are involved with a crazymaker, or suspect that you yourself are one, it is important that you admit it. If your crazymaker is using you, admit that you yourself are using your crazymaker. It is a block you have chosen yourself, to deter your creative trajectory. As much as you are being exploited, you are using your crazymaker to block your own creative flow. Pick up a book on codependency, or join a twelve-step program to thwart the crazymaker's tortured tango. Al-Anon and Sex and Love Addicts Anonymous are excellent programs for breaking the crazymaker's hold on you. The next time you catch yourself thinking, "He/She is driving me crazy," ask yourself what creative work you are trying to block by your involvement.

TOXIC FRIENDS

The phone rang and I answered it. The caller was another writer, officially a friend.

"Are you writing? You're always writing," my caller began the call.

"I'm writing," I allowed. "I'm halfway through a book."

"Good for you. I've got eighty pages of I don't know what."

"That's eighty pages of something, I'm sure."

"Your voice to God's ear. What's your book about?"

Now comes the big question:
What are you going to write
about? And the equally big
answer: Anything you damn
well want.

—STEPHEN KING

"Writing."

"Writing? There's lots of books on writing. What's your hook?"

"My hook?"

"What makes you think your book will sell? Have you got a deal?"

"I'm writing it on spec," I volunteered.

"That's risky. And your topic . . ."

My officially friendly friend didn't sound very friendly.

"I think it's a good topic," I mustered.

"If you think so," my caller continued.

Now I was defensive. "I've enjoyed writing it so far."

"You're an optimist."

"I always enjoy writing."

"I do too, when I've got a deal. Has your agent tried to sell it yet?"

"We're waiting until I'm finished. About two more months."

"That's if you don't get stuck. You can't afford writer's block."

"No," I agreed. "I can't."

"Well, I was just checking on you," my caller ended the call. "You'll let me know how it goes."

I got off the call feeling slimed. The exchange had been toxic. My caller was competitive. I felt my joy on the project not-so-subtly trashed. The lurking subtext of the call had been "consider the odds against your success." For me, thinking about the odds was a sip of poison. As an antidote, I needed to talk to someone positive—and fast. I dialed my friend, writer Jacob Nordby.

"Mercy!" Jacob exclaimed when I detailed my poisonous call. He bolstered my wounded writer, saying simply, "Your book is good. Fresh."

"I got discouraged," I confessed.

"Your caller was negative," Jacob stated firmly. "You can't afford to be. You have a book to finish."

"What if I get writer's block?" I whined.

"You're not going to get writer's block. You're on a roll."

"Thank you."

"No need to thank me. Just keep writing."

"Thanks anyhow." And we got off the phone.

Jacob is for me a believing mirror. He is positive, optimistic, cheerful. He believes in me and my work. My toxic caller, by contrast, was a funhouse mirror, reflecting me and my work in a distorted way. Officially a friend, my caller was anything but friendly. Passive aggressive, undercutting my confidence like a bad fairy from a fairy tale.

"Your caller was negative." I recalled Jacob's words. "You can't afford to be. You have a book to finish."

Yes, I do have a book to finish. Writing out the poisonous call, I resolve to avoid the caller in the future. Not a friend, rather, an enemy, toxic to me and my work.

DOUBT

"Begin where you are," I have often written. Taking my own advice, I write that I am at writing station one: the library, seated in my big leather writing chair. I'm set to write an essay on doubt, and I doubt that I'll be able to pull it off. Pen to page, I write, "Doubt is excruciating." This is no lie. I am experiencing doubt now, and it is queasy-making. Doubt, self-doubt, is a vote of confidence in the critic. My Nigel whispers to me, "You have nothing valid to say," and I believe it. Instead of having confidence in my talent and my history, I mistrust myself, doubting my worth.

"What you are writing now, it sounds stupid," my Nigel hisses. And so I cast about, looking for a better way to say, "Doubt is sickening." But doubt *is* sickening. A vote of confidence in the devil. An experience that all writers undergo.

Let us say you have been writing well. Doubt will whisper, "Do you sound cocky?" Self-confidence is an insult to doubt. "Maybe you should try again," Perfectionism rears its head.

"What I have done is good enough," our rational mind retorts. "Perhaps it's not perfect, but it is good."

"Are you sure?" Doubt whispers. And of course we're not sure, faced with doubt. Doubt is insidious. It undercuts our confidence with sly innuendos. If we are bold, speaking in our own behalf, doubt tells us that is hubris. If we cave in to anxiety, doubt would have us doubt further still.

The wind of inspiration dies in the face of doubt. Make no mistake: doubt is powerful. It pokes into the hidden corners of our mind, saying, "But have you considered *this*?" Doubt has our second thoughts, and our third and our fourth. Forget our good experience with trusting our first thoughts. Doubt tells us that experience was a fluke. Let us say we muster our courage and stand up to doubt. Not to be easily vanquished, doubt whispers that our newly found confidence is a "mistake."

"You're the mistake," we rally our defenses, doubting our doubts. Doubt wobbles in the face of our confidence. Doubt is a bully, after all, and like all bullies it backs down when confronted.

"I believe I may be right," we modestly say. Doubt cannot survive the light that modesty casts.

"I believe I'm certain," we finally assert. Faced with our calm certitude, doubt vanishes.

AFFIRMATIONS

Rain spits against the window. The day is gray and drear. So are my Morning Pages. Many times, people ask me about the "negativity" of their Morning Pages. They are afraid that if they write their negative feelings, they will somehow perpetuate or increase them. I explain to them—gently—that they are "ventilating" their negative feelings, not increasing them. Many times, Morning Pages nudge us into facing an unpleasant truth. "I need to get sober," "I need to get divorced," "I need to look for a new job," "I need to exercise." Morning Pages are a tough-love friend. They urge us to be more honest, to take action where it is needed, and, in the words of the Serenity Prayer—"God, grant me the serenity to accept the things I cannot change, the courage to change the things I can, and the wisdom to know the difference."

Pen to the page, we sort our life into workable categories. At the pages' urging, we face our demons, and when we do, we find we have room—on the page and in our lives—for new and positive endeavors. Having ventilated our darker feelings, we move toward the light, and one of the most effective ways to do this is through the use of affirmations.

Affirmations are positive statements of positive beliefs. They work like levers to pry loose our lingering negatives. Affirmations often sound like wishful thinking. Let us say you want to lose weight. Your affirmation might read, "I am trim and slender." A glance in the mirror tells us this is not so—yet. Affirmations specialize in the "yets." We write, "I am sober and happy." We find that we become willing to embrace sobriety and joy.

A daily practice of affirmations is a powerful tool, particularly as applied to areas where we feel stuck. "I am loved and lovable," we may write when we despair of our lovability. The act of putting positive statements onto the page pries loose the stranglehold of despair. "I am solvent," we may write when our finances are in need of repair. Soon enough, we find ourselves prosperous. Our affirmation has curbed our tendency to overspend and under-save. Using affirmations is an excursion into open-mindedness. Affirmations are not wishful thinking. Rather, they are a bridge we ourselves construct to a sunnier future. Outside my window, the storm clouds part and a rainbow arches, triumphant over the gloom.

TASKS

1. U-turns: List the following categories: Music, Film/Theater, Visual arts, Public speaking/Performance, and Crafts. Next to each one, note a U-turn you have made. What happened? When and why did you stop working in the art form, however subtly? Now, write down a tiny action you could take towards reversing your U-turn. Could you choose one action from your list and take it?

2. Anger: Number from one to ten and list ten angers. Remember, anger is fuel. When you are finished, look through your list. Does it suggest an action you could take? Can you use the energy of anger for good?

3. Toxic Friends/Crazymakers: We all have toxic friends and crazymakers in our lives at one time or another. Fill in the following:

   Three crazymakers I have known are:
   The worst thing a crazymaker has done to me is:
   I suspect I was involved with this person because:

   A toxic friend in my life right now is:
   A way I could distance myself from this negativity is:

4. Deadlines: Take pen in hand and write for five minutes about deadlines. How do you feel about them? Do they have a positive, negative, or neutral connotation? Were there times when deadlines

helped you? Times when you felt they hurt you? Now, look at your current project. Could you make a healthy deadline for yourself, based on your daily quota, for when you will finish your first draft?

5. Affirmations: Quickly list three fears in relation to your project. Now, convert each into a positive affirmation. For example: "I'm afraid I will never finish my project" becomes "I easily and happily bring my project to its ideal completion." Work with your affirmations this week by writing them out each day after your Morning Pages.

CHECK IN

1. How many days did you do your Morning Pages this week? Are you able to get to them quickly and do them without interruption or distraction?

2. Did you take your Artist Date? What was it? How was it? Did you experience synchronicity, optimism, or a sense of a benevolent higher power? All three?

3. Did you take your walks? Are you able to do them alone and without distraction? Did you try walking out with a question and seeing if you returned home with an answer?

4. Did you hit your daily quota? How many pages are you into your project? Do you feel a sense of excitement as you watch your page count building?

DISMANTLE YOUR PERFECTIONIST

Over the decades that I have taught writers and artists of all stripes, I have seen perfectionism to be one of the most common of all blocks. Perfectionism threatens to stop us in our tracks, it makes us question ourselves and our ideas, and it argues that our limiting beliefs must be true. This week, you will dismantle your perfectionism, revealing that, like a schoolyard bully, it retreats when you stand up to it. You will work with one of my most radical tools, Media Deprivation—which also produces some of the most radical results in eradicating creative blocks. You will be guided to be gentle with yourself as you move through this week. Remember, treating yourself like a precious object will make you strong.

ORIGINALITY

It's a gray day. Many tiny white clouds spatter the sky. My thoughts are scattered too. It's a day for mulling, turning over in my mind common writers' complaints.

"Julia, I want to be original," I am often told. The desire to be original is actually wrongheaded. I would dare to say there is no such thing as being original. Perhaps all stories have been told before. How much wiser it would be if people said, "Julia, I want to be authentic." The desire to be original comes from the ego. It is the ego's desire to be special. The desire to be authentic comes from the soul. It is the soul's desire to be honest. When we examine the idea of originality, we recognize that the work which resonates for us is not so much original as it is heartfelt. It is not that we have never before heard an idea; rather that the idea resonates with our heart.

"But Julia, everything I have to say has been said before. There is nothing new."

Where do we get the idea that our work must be new, that it must say something no one has previously said? If we reflect for a moment on the work that moves us, we will realize that it is not "newness" that moves us. We are moved instead by our recognition of the human condition. In other words, not something new, but something familiar.

The great teacher Joseph Campbell taught us that myth resonated due to its echoing of stories of the past. According to Campbell, there are no "new" stories, only the new telling of stories that we know and love. *West Side Story,* that great musical, was a retelling of a Shakespearean masterpiece. *Star Wars,* that epic film, has its roots in myth. Perhaps all stories are stories we have heard before, and our pleasure lies as much in their retelling as their telling. The accurate telling of a tale moves us because of its accuracy. As we seek the vulnerability to write the details of our personal lives, we write the universal, and the universal cannot fail to move us. But the ego resists such a simple directive.

"But Julia, my story has been told before," the ego yelps. Yes, it has, and that is what gives it its power. As we admit on the page our faults and foibles, we allow the reader to identify, to enter the story we are telling. When a work lacks resonance, it is because it lacks vulnerability. It takes humility, not ego, to be a great writer.

"But Julia, surely it takes ego to tell a tale." Far more than ego, it takes courage, the necessary courage to say the familiar, knowing that it has been said before, and that it will be said again, and that the saying, the authentic trac-

One day I will find the right words, and they will be simple.

—JACK KEROUAC

ing of our tale, is what makes us original. And yes, we all have tales to tell.

Many of us believe that our lives are boring, that they do not hold material for our work. But our lives are not boring, and they do hold material for our work. At its root, the fear of being "boring" is a fear of not being original. We forget that "original" has as its root the word "origin," and we are the *origin* of our work, which is, by definition, original, not boring.

As we labor to be the originating point of our efforts, we find ourselves becoming more honest. Our honesty translates into what we mistakenly call "originality." In striving to have a voice, we must ask ourselves the right question, and that is, "Am I being fully, authentically myself?" When we can answer "yes" to this query, we can rest assured that our work will resonate for others. It is here that I take issue with the expression "familiarity breeds contempt." Instead, we find that familiarity breeds respect. As our work reminds our reader of prior work, it gains—not loses—credibility.

Originality is the net result of honesty and authenticity.

LIMITING BELIEFS

"Writing is difficult," our mythology goes. "Writers themselves are tormented beings."

Our cultural assumptions might have us believe that writers are drunk, lost, lonely, self-destructive. It is important that we examine this mythology. With beliefs like this, is it any wonder that we hesitate to take to the page?

But what if these deep-seated beliefs are wrong? What if writers are actually user-friendly? Blocked writers are those who suffer and cause suffering to their intimates. Writers who write regularly keep their demons at bay. A habit of daily writing brings contentment and even happiness. Writers who write are at peace with themselves, and at peace with their fellows.

It matters less *what* you write than *that* you write. Morning Pages allow us to let off steam. Think of a tea kettle building up pressure. When we tip the kettle and allow water to flow, the built-up pressure is siphoned off. So it is with daily writing. As we allow our words to flow to the page, we experience relief and satisfaction.

"But Julia, writers are broke," I am sometimes told. This, by someone hovering at the shore. Again, I would say blocked writers are broke. The writers who allow themselves the freedom to take to the page are often reimbursed monetarily for their risk-taking.

Best-selling author Elizabeth Gilbert worked the Artist's Way and reaped rewards, creative and monetary. "Without the Artist's Way," she wrote to me, "there would be no *Eat Pray Love*." But there was the Artist's Way, and the bestselling book it spawned, a book that sold millions.

I was recently approached as I sat writing in a cafe. "You're Julia Cameron, aren't you," inquired a fellow diner. "I just want to thank you. I worked the Artist's Way program, and as a result, wrote and published a book of my own. Just this afternoon I did a publicity shoot for it. Using your tools, I put my own thoughts to the page, and now I'm being paid for them."

I tell this story to illustrate my point: when we write for love, we often earn money. I have written several dozen books, many of them on spec, and most of them have been written for love, not money. *The Artist's Way* itself was written as a manifesto. It was intended to free the creativity of its readers. Initially self-published, it was mailed out to many who learned of its existence through word of mouth. The initial hand-bound book sold for twenty dollars—five dollars more than the "officially" published edition.

All that I hope to say in books, all that I ever hope to say, is that I love the world.

—E. B. WHITE

As the popularity of *The Artist's Way* spread, I began to hear more and more stories of monies earned by the publications of our students. Sometimes the monies they brought in were substantial. Bert wrote a book about money, and its lively sales filled his coffers. "I took a risk and it paid off," he says. "And I do mean paid."

Martin Scorsese, a hardheaded artist, had this assessment: "For those who will use it, it is a valuable tool to get in touch with their own creativity." Such accolades were heartfelt, and I received them gladly. I still do.

Today's mail brought me a thank-you note. "Thank you so much for your book," the note read. "Thanks to your tools, I am completing a novel, and I now know that I am a real artist."

I keep a file for such notes. They reinforce my conviction that artists need encouragement, and I am happy to provide it.

Morning Pages consistently challenge my students to confront the beliefs they have about the artist's life. Facing down negative mythology moves them into optimism and action.

MEDIA DEPRIVATION

The day is balmy. I take advantage of the warmth to sit outside on the patio of my favored restaurant, Santa Fe Bar & Grill. My dining companion is another writer, but she is not writing.

"I think you need to go on a diet," I tell her while we are studying the menus.

"I'm already skinny," she protests. And she is.

"I'm not suggesting you count calories," I tell her. "I'm suggesting you count words. What you need, to get started again, is a week of media deprivation," I explain.

All of us have a daily quota of words. We read them, we speak them, we listen to them. How we use them is up to us. When we are writing, we sometimes overspend our quota and find ourselves stuck. We no longer have words to say. And it is when we run out of words that we need to employ a special trick. That trick is something I call Media Deprivation.

Rather than use—and abuse—our daily quota of words, we deprive ourselves of words. The result is that words begin to build up, creating a pressure that eventually spills onto the page. Media deprivation is a potent tool. It means just what it says: no media. Yes, that means no reading and no time spent on the computer. It even means no talk radio. For all of us, there is a panic which sets in. No words? No words! No magazines, no books, no computers, no words. Forbidden, words call to us. We are banning words, and the forbidden words begin to build up a head of steam. We are all addicted to words, and when words are forbidden, we find ourselves restless, irritable, and discontent. We miss our words. We are tempted to cheat, to read just a little. But not reading pays off. We sense its wisdom.

Mimi found herself stalled halfway across a play. "It was going so well," she moaned. "I was writing so fast." She sounded wistful and a little vain. Her speed was something she was proud of. Bingeing on writing, she had overfished her well.

"Try media deprivation," I urged her. "No reading of any kind. No words."

"No words?" she gasped.

"No words," I told her firmly, explaining that as she gave up the words of others, her own words would come back to her. And so, she embarked on her literary fast. Despite her skepticism, she found herself ready to write again within a week.

"Thank you for this tool," she told me excitedly. "I was afraid I was stalled for good."

The role of a writer is not to say what we can all say, but what we are unable to say.

—ANAÏS NIN

Our need to write is very strong, but no stronger than the tool of media deprivation.

Richard, a seasoned novelist, abruptly lost his voice. He had been writing steadily and well, but in his excitement about the book, he began to binge on writing, overfishing his inner well.

"I'm out of ideas," Richard complained. "I'm out of words." I urged him, like Mimi, to try a week of media deprivation.

"I'm afraid I'll never write again," Richard told me.

"You'll write, and write well," I assured him. "Think of media deprivation as a rest."

"I'm afraid to try it," Richard confessed. "I'm afraid that if I stop writing, stop trying to write, I'll never start again."

"You're just being dramatic," I teased him. "Give the tool a try."

"I haven't got any better ideas," Richard admitted. "And so I'll try it. But tell me, do you really mean no reading?"

"Yes," I said.

"No Google?" Richard queried.

"No Google," I said firmly. And so, Richard launched into a week without words. He found himself tempted to cheat, to read the phone book, to read anything at all. But I urged him to be vigilant and strict with himself. "No NPR."

"Now I know what's next," he phoned me excitedly to say a week later. His week of media deprivation had paid off. He was thrilled.

"I told you the tool would work," I responded.

Richard and Mimi are now both devotees of media deprivation. They are not alone. It is often the artists who resist this tool the most who gain the most benefit from trying it. I have had lyricists tell me that, without using a rhyming website for a week, their imaginations have stretched in exciting and surprising directions.

I am often asked—pointedly, I might add—how to deal with having a job where it is important to respond to emails in a timely way, and where reading is required? My answer is this: first of all, I teach adults, and I am not suggesting that you shirk your responsibilities in a way that is self-destructive. I am, however, asking that you cut out reading as much as you possibly can—and what I have found, over and over, is that there are many ways to do this. In every life, there is an "excess" of words, media, television, texting, surfing the internet, that, when avoided for a week, releases a great deal of self-empowerment and creative energy. So, I say, if it's something that can't wait, of course, you deal with it—and try to deal with it using as few words as you can. But if it can wait . . . let it wait. The reward of media deprivation is a positive—and often prodigious—flow of words. I love to write, and so I love this tool.

TREATING YOURSELF LIKE A PRECIOUS OBJECT

It's a blue and white day with white puffy clouds and wind lashing the piñon tree. The turbulent day requires stamina. Many tasks loom ahead. All of us wish we were stronger, able to accomplish the day's tasks with ease. We strain to meet the day's demands. We will ourselves to have strength. But all our willpower avails us nothing. We are going about our exertions backwards. Striving for strength, we feel our weakness. We flog ourselves forward, pressuring ourselves to accomplish more. Faced with a day's writing, we doubt our inspiration. Words come in a trickle, not a flood. And so we push harder, striving for energy, but encountering fatigue. Isn't there a better way? Must the answer always be "try harder"?

I think there is a better way, and that is to be gentle with yourself. Lower your expectations of the day. Instead of demanding more, demand less. Set the bar low. Divide the number of expected tasks by two. Take heed of the mantra "easy does it." Better yet, consider this adage: "Treating yourself like a precious object will make you strong."

How would you treat a precious object? Treat yourself that way. Do not demand of yourself more than you can comfortably accomplish. Feel your stores of energy. Are you asking more than your reserves allow? Writing requires energy. Recognize that fact. Do not ask yourself to write more than a low, doable quota. You will find that as you demand less, you will in fact be able to write more. As you stop straining, you will enjoy a more fluid flow. Your day's work will seem less like work as you begin to find writing a pleasurable activity.

Treating yourself like a precious object requires attention and practice. Be alert to the ways you abuse yourself. Do you get enough sleep? Are you eating well? Do you listen to your body when it says "rest now"? As you learn to husband your energies, you will find yourself with energy at day's end. Treating yourself like a precious object will have paid off as you find stores of unexpected stamina.

The day has turned to gray. I have written my way easily from clear weather to storm. Treating myself like a precious object, I head to bed for an afternoon's nap. My body is saying "rest now," and I obey.

BRIBES

I don't know about you, but my writer is easily bribed. When I am stalled, I offer my writer a reward for going forward. The reward—a polite word for "bribe"—can be material or behavioral. My writer has a fondness for

Just write a little bit every day. Even if it's for only half an hour—write, write, write.

—MADELEINE L'ENGLE

chai lattes, and so I say, "Just finish up this essay and I'll take you to the coffee shop for a chai latte and a piece of cherry pie."

If the piece of writing to be done is small, the bribe can be small. If I need to write longer, the bribe can be larger: "I'll buy you that navy blue polka dot dress." There are those who think of the bribe as "cheating"—"Write ten minutes and you can have that chocolate bar"—but I am a working writer, and I use whatever works. Bribes work. Cherry pie and lattes got me through an entire book. An essay at a time, a bribe at a time. The polka dot dress was the reward for finishing a second draft. When I wear it, I feel "writerly." My reward for a job well done is tangible. I love to write, and I love my dress.

Purists insist that a bribe should itself be writerly: a fancy new fountain pen that makes writing a pleasure, a handsome journal for ninety days' worth of Morning Pages. My friend Suzanne Sealy collects costly fountain pens. She fills journal after journal with bold script.

"I love to write," she tells me, and her writing is fine calligraphy, her pens working as bribes. They feel good to her hand.

I don't use a fountain pen. I use a uni-ball 207, a fast-writing pen that I buy by the batch, four to a packet. "Finish this essay and you can have a new pen," I tell myself. The bribe works. My writer *loves* a new pen.

"Finish a draft of this book and I'll buy you a whole new outfit," I offer when inspiration is low. My writer perks up. A "whole new outfit" is worth the toil of writing. I love to write, and my writer loves a good bribe.

CONNECTION

I open my mailbox to find a brightly colored card featuring stargazer lilies, my favorite flowers. It is a note from Emma Lively, who lives thousands of miles away in

Brooklyn. The card reads, "Dear Julie, Stargazers always remind me of you! Love, Emma." I take the card inside and add it with a lily magnet to my refrigerator door. I am grateful for the colorful card and more grateful for the note.

We write to express ourselves, but we also write to connect. Connection is a primary human need. From cave dwellers onward, we scratched our message into stone, hoping that it would be read and understood. As we became more adroit at expression, the messages that we sent became more complex. "I am here and you are there," our messages began, meaning, our relationship to one another. From there, we went on to express our feelings. "I am here and you are there, and this is how I feel about that." As time progressed, our messages grew in complexity. We became better able to express nuances and shades of meaning. In time, we were able to connect with great accuracy, and we experienced this connection with relief.

The human urge to bond was the driving force behind our messages. Our connection became everyday, matter-of-fact as we expressed ourselves more and more fully. The urge to connect remains a paramount human desire. "I am here and you are there, and we are in this world together." We write to acknowledge and strengthen our bond. Our connection is primal.

As artists, we must also connect with other artists. We connect through our art, and we connect artist-to-artist. I am reading a novel, *Rio Bardo,* written by my friend Logan Sven Peterson. The book is rich in flora and fauna, showcasing Logan's eye for detail. Yesterday I ran into Logan unexpectedly. "I'm halfway through your book," I told him. "You're a wonderful writer."

He flushed at the compliment. "It always throws me to know someone is actually reading the book," he confessed.

"I'm reading it and enjoying it. Your eye for detail is marvelous."

"Thank you. That means a lot. It's time for me to be promoting the book, and I find that while I loved writing it, I hate promoting it."

"I can understand that," I told him. "But you're a real writer's writer. I think you need to remember that when faced with promoting your work."

"Your voice to God's ear!" he exclaimed. "I truly did love the process of writing."

I thought of my friend Natalie Goldberg and her palpable love of writing. She was headed off for five weeks as writer-in-residence at a retreat center just off the coast from Seattle. Her voice held scarcely banked excitement as she told me, "They're giving me a house and a car and nothing to do for five weeks but write. I can't wait." Natalie and I have been friends for twenty-five years. We admire each other's work and we egg each other on into new work. A survivor of leukemia, Natalie recently wrote a book on cancer. "My agent had a devilishly hard time selling it. The topic was too dark. But sell it she did, to Shambala Publications, the press that published my first book, *Writing Down the Bones*. I didn't get much money, but I wanted the book to see the light of day."

With her cancer book safely sold, Natalie is free to turn to other topics. She wants to write a book about Japan and her recent travels there. Perhaps her five weeks as writer-in-residence would give her a start. It gives me a sense of community and camaraderie to know what my writer friends are working on.

Email has given us an easy way to connect. My girlfriend Sonia Choquette recently moved from Chicago to Paris. I missed her terribly, until I received an email detailing her Paris life. I emailed her back, detailing my life in Santa Fe.

"Goody, let's stay in touch by email," Sonia shot back.

And so we did. Letters take a long time to arrive, while email is instant. We connect with our friends and colleagues instantaneously. We spell out our messages and then press "send." Delivery happens in a flash. We are connected.

There are those who oppose email, but I consider it a happy invention, a flashback to the days when British mail was delivered multiple times daily, making letters a nearly instant form of communication. I recently spent an evening with a docent from the Georgia O'Keeffe Museum. She told me of O'Keeffe's voluminous correspondence with her lover, then husband, Alfred Stieglitz. Theirs was a passionate romance fueled by the written word.

A sun sign Scorpio, the most passionate of astrological signs, O'Keeffe wrote to Stieglitz with urgency. Visitors to the museum got a glimpse of her radiant sensuality.

"Only connect," poet Theodore Roethke is said to have remarked, and O'Keeffe took his advice with a vengeance.

"The letters were *hot*," the docent marveled, "and they wrote thousands." Georgia O'Keeffe's flower paintings communicated her passionate nature. But her letters communicated even more.

It's a stormy night and darkness descends swiftly. I perch at my dining room table lit by a crystal chandelier. I write out cards to my far-flung friends. One friend in particular engages me. I find myself straying from friendship into romance.

"I miss you," I write. "How soon can we see each other?" My friend and I live a thousand miles apart. Our cards cross in the mail. We are tiptoeing into intimacy, a word at a time. We will rendezvous in a month. Until then, our passion will remain written, a carefully banked fire. This morning's mail brought me a card. "Love," it was signed. Reading it, I feel a spark of connection.

We write to taste life twice, in the moment and in retrospect.

—ANAÏS NIN

MEETING WITH A FELLOW WRITER

Every Thursday night at 6:00 P.M., I meet my friend and fellow writer Nick Kapustinsky for dinner. I say we meet for dinner, but the meal is secondary. We meet to exchange poetry, each of us bringing a new poem for the other's scrutiny. Nick is a fine poet, and his work lightens the meal. Last week's poem detailed a lover lost. He wrote:

> *Liminal cliffs and impossible moats*
> *That is where I loved you most.*
> *Now I sit with standing grass*
> *And wait for stubborn dreams to pass.*

Nick's poem captures the loss he felt, losing a beloved lover. I order grilled salmon and shove my poem across the table. It is a brief poem, five lines in all, beginning, "The stars at night are not so near as far . . ."

Nick reads my poem thoughtfully, enjoying the tight rhyme scheme. We raise the bar: next week we will bring three poems, two old, one new. During COVID our meals were interrupted and the poems piled up. We are striving now to get current on a year's banked writing. Nick, a hiker, climbed Santa Fe's mountains during the pandemic. He wrote of them with a muscular grace. I find I love his mountain poems, and eagerly anticipate more. Waiting for my salmon, I read Nick's poem aloud.

"You're such a fine reader, you always make my poems sound better than they are," Nick comments.

"Nonsense," I tell him. "They *are* good."

My salmon arrives and we lapse into silence, eating. I am fond of our restaurant, the Santa Fe Bar & Grill. Nick enjoys steak tacos and flash-fried oysters. They are savory, like his poem.

Nick and I have been friends five years, bonded by

You can make anything by writing.

—C. S. LEWIS

our love of writing—and each other's writing. Sometimes I will read him an essay I take pride in. Nick listens intently, so quiet I fear he is bored. But no, he is simply focused. His comments later show his rapt attention.

Nick and I often work together, helping each other respond to emails, crafting writerly replies. Our joint prose is crisp. We are, if not terse, brief and to the point. Writing on my own, without Nick as a sounding board, I catch myself thinking, "What would Nick say here?"

On holidays, we exchange books, selecting with care something we think the other will like. Nick is widely read in contemporary American poetry. His choice of books is far-ranging, frequently introducing me to a poet I haven't read.

Have I said that Nick is a fine actor as well as a writer? I find the words of my plays fit easily in his mouth. During COVID, we did a Zoom production of my play *Love in the DMZ*. Nick played the male lead, a soldier in Vietnam. Our audience numbered many Vietnam veterans, who were unanimous in applauding Nick's performance. The play met with fine reviews, singling out his skill. As the author, I was thrilled to watch my character come to life in his hands. I posted the production on my website, juliacameronlive.com.

"You make me look good," I told Nick.

"You make *me* look good," he echoed me. Friends, colleagues, collaborators, we are happy in each other's company. As artists we relish the support. Thursday cannot come again too quickly.

TAKING BREAKS

The wind in the piñon tree is gentle today, after several days of intense velocity, lashing its branches to and fro. The gentle wind comes as a relief. Calm rules the day. Calm rules my writing, as well. After half a week of writing flat out, an essay a day, I, too, am ready for a breather. I know too well the strain of pushing ahead. I know too well the symptoms of overwork. Exhaustion makes writing difficult, and so I have learned to halt and take a break before exhaustion sets in.

I wasn't always so wise. As a young writer I attacked my projects with grim determination. I pushed ahead day after day, ignoring the telltale signs of creative fatigue. At first I wrote well, and then, after flogging myself forward to continue despite the cost, my writing became "thin," forced with the strain of too much and too often. I would write until I was exhausted. My writing suffered from overexertion—and yet—and still—I whipped myself forward.

It was years into my writing career that I learned to pay attention to my spirit's need for a break. I was writing a novel, *The Dark Room,* and the writing went well—until it didn't. I stretched and strained to capture the novel's forward momentum. Why, I wondered, was the novel suddenly so difficult? I say "suddenly," although the signs of fatigue were obvious, if only I cared to pay attention. Instead, I pushed on, as my language flattened out and images became elusive. Despite my best efforts, my writing ground to a halt. I had overfished my inner well. I needed a break.

Discouraged and dismayed, I set my novel aside. I beat myself up that I "lacked the stamina" to finish it. I put myself on a recuperative regime. Not writing, I took myself on brief creative excursions: Artist Dates, as I called them. Day by day, I felt my energy returning. My dark mood lifted. One day, I felt ready to one more time tackle my novel. My days off had restored my spirits, and with them, my ability to write. I one more time put pen to page, but with a difference: my fallow period—writer's block—had scared me. I set back to work on the novel at a moderate pace. No more flat-out writing for me. I paid attention now to my symptoms of overexertion. Instead of flogging myself forward, I was gentle with myself. I resolved to take regular Artist Dates to restore my inner well. Working temperately, my novel blossomed under my hand. I finished it. I sold it. And I thanked it. It had taught me the wisdom of "easy does it." I now knew it meant "easy accomplishes it," and not just "slow down."

I set my pen down now, deciding to take a solo drive—one of my favorite types of breaks.

The climb from the valley floor to the mountain peaks is steep and curvy—so steep and so curvy that the speed limit is posted at ten miles per hour. I'm driving to the peaks to enjoy the aspen groves, turned bright gold with the autumn chill. From below, the fiery gold peaks are a bright patchwork quilt draped over the mountains. Their season is brief—a scant two weeks. I have learned to go early lest I miss their glory.

The lower slopes are evergreen, juniper, and piñon. Only as I climb to the heights do the aspen appear in all their golden radiance. "Thank you, God," I breathe, taking in their glory. The trees are golden spears piercing the azure sky. Prayers of praise are the natural response to their beauty. Driving into their midst, the car enters a cathedral, fiery spires reach to the heavens. The forest floor is a golden carpet. The tall trees shed their leaves in a fiery cascade.

"Hosannah in the highest," my heart leaps up. The grandeur of the grove provokes ecstatic praise. The afternoon light filters through the trees with spokes of fire. I find myself humbled by the beauty all around me. Awe touches my soul.

The Great Creator is showing off. Majesty speaks of the godhead. Beauty is a gateway to the divine and this particular beauty calls for a worshipful heart. "Glory to God in the highest," the heart declares. Exaltation fills the spirit. Joy rules the day. I do not think it's possible

Words bounce. Words, if you let them, will do what they want to do and what they have to do.

—ANNE CARSON

to behold this beauty without turning one's thoughts to its maker. Even an atheist's heart would be opened to the divine.

Leaving the grove, the sense of wonder lingers. Descending the steep curves to the valley floor, the heart remains bedazzled. Surely such beauty has its roots in divinity. I feel both calm and energized; my inner well is filled.

Back at home, notebook in hand, I glance out the window to see the piñon tree bobbing gently in the wind. I turn my hand to finishing this essay. Instead of straining forward, I pause. In the pause, words come to me.

DEALING WITH REJECTION

Today at lunch I sat with a marvelous writer who had just received a rejection by a renowned publisher. He knew his book was good; it had already been published once by a small press, to fine reviews. Now he sought broader publication. The book deserved it. He was grieved by the rejection, but he also was curious. He knew that when the universe closed one door, it often opened another. His agent would make further submissions. He had hoped for an early win, but was prepared for the long haul.

I told him about the journey of my own novel, *Mozart's Ghost*. It endured forty-three rejections before two presses in a row wanted to pick it up. I explained to him that, throughout the lengthy submissions process, I had enjoyed the faith of my good friend and believing mirror, Sonia Choquette. Each time the book was rejected, Sonia would respond, "I see this book getting published." Her optimism was stubborn, and gave me the courage not to give up. I wished for my friend the same courage.

"I'll be your believing mirror," I volunteered to my friend. "I see your book also getting published. It's just a matter of time."

The best work that anybody ever writes is the work that is on the verge of embarrassing him, always.

—ARTHUR MILLER

"You're such an optimist," my friend exclaimed, but I demurred.

"I'm not an optimist, I'm a realist. And realistically, yours is a fine book. It will find its way." I told my friend I had learned the same lesson. When I wrote *The Artist's Way*, I showed the manuscript to my movie agent, and she remarked, "Oh, Julia, there's no market for a book on creativity. Go back to writing screenplays; that's where you're successful." Like my novelist friend, I knew the book was good. And so, I let go of my prestigious agent and took a flyer that the universe was in charge, and somehow the book would sell. This took courage, more courage than I felt I had. I trusted, but what had I done? I was never without doubt. I wailed to my boyfriend, "I'm worried I'm being self-destructive, firing my agent."

"Nonsense," my boyfriend replied, "the book is good, and I have the phone number of another agent, Susan Schulman."

"I'm afraid to call her," I protested, and I was.

"I'll make the call for you," he said, and dialed the number, launching into a spiel about the greatness of the book.

"Every year at Christmas, I get a wonderful book," Susan Schulman told him. "So, send me your manuscript. Maybe this year yours is it." We mailed the manuscript to Susan Schulman and waited on pins and needles. What if she agreed that the book was unsaleable?

Christmas came and went. The day after the New Year, my phone rang. It was Susan Schulman, who wanted to represent the book. "That sounds great," my boyfriend enthused, handing me the line.

"I'd love to represent you," Susan said. "I think I know just where this book should be published."

And so, we agreed that she should handle the book. Two weeks later she had a sale: Jeremy P. Tarcher, the brilliant publisher who ran America's foremost creativity press, wanted to buy *The Artist's Way*.

And so I found myself optimistic about the fate of my friend's novel. As he ladled navy bean soup—comfort food—to his mouth, I ladled comforting thoughts to his ear.

"Your book is great," I told him. "I myself have read it three times. Somebody wonderful will want to pick it up. Don't give up."

My friend spooned up the last of his soup. "Your voice to God's ear," he remarked. I thought to myself that God's ear was cocked, listening for the news of a fine novel. It would be published, as it deserved.

THE WALL

It's a sunny, blue and white day—a day for enthusiasm. All is going well, and so I reflect, it is always this way at the beginning. Writing begins with enthusiasm. We launch into a project with optimism. We have an idea, we trust our ability to execute it, we set about putting it to the page. All goes swimmingly for a time—until we hit The Wall. The Wall occurs, in most writing, about two-thirds of the way into our work. Put simply, The Wall is doubt. Our previously good idea suddenly seems suspect. We doubt its validity. We doubt our own abilities. This doubt is a knife edge we turn upon ourselves. Our writing skids to a halt.

"Julia, I feel such doubt, it stops me in my tracks," I have been told many times. I sympathize. Doubt is an excruciatingly painful feeling. It tempts us to take creative U-turns, abandoning our work.

"Julia, it was going so well, and then I found myself thinking, 'What if I'm kidding myself?'" That is the voice of doubt. It whispers that we are without talent, and that our hopes of success are mere grandiosity. It encourages us to mistrust our perceptions. The Wall towers high.

Typically, when we encounter The Wall, we attempt to power our way past it and over it. "It *is* a good idea," we say to ourselves defensively. "I *know* it's a good idea." But our forced optimism doesn't win the day. The Wall still towers, casting its ominous shadow on our work. We are like convicts in a prison yard. We are tempted to despair. The Wall is winning—we cannot scale its height. But no! There is a better way to conquer The Wall, and that is to burrow under it. Instead of trying to convince ourselves of the brilliance of our idea, we need to say instead, "I am willing to finish this piece of work even if my idea is terrible." In other words, "I am willing to write badly."

The moment we are willing to write badly, we begin to have freedom. The Wall no longer dominates our emotional landscape. Instead, like convicts striving to escape prison, we do well not by scrambling over The Wall, but by digging our way to freedom under it. Most of us find this approach to The Wall a novel idea. We are not really willing to write badly, and yet, when we give ourselves permission, we find that by being willing to write badly, we may write very well indeed. We certainly write well enough to finish our project. The Wall crumples when faced with our tenacity. The Wall cannot withstand our subversive approach. We win by being willing to lose. "I'm willing to write badly" wins us freedom.

DELIGHT

I'll begin where I am: in the library, in my writing chair, scanning the room for inspiration. There! I've settled on a photograph of my late father, cradling his little black Scottie, playfully named Blue (as in the folk song). *I had an old dog, and his name was Blue. Bet you five dollars he's a good dog too.* In the photo, my father looks fiercely protective. In the photo, little Blue looks fiercely protective. They were a team, guarding and guiding each other. They lived together aboard my father's sailboat, anchored off Longboat Key, Florida. It was a delightful mooring. Colorful parrots flocked in the palm trees bordering the marina. Vivid flowers—pink, orange, and red—lined the pathways. My father, no gardener himself, enjoyed their blooms. His brief letters noted their beauty.

Living on my ranch in New Mexico, I wrote him near daily, detailing the beauty and perfume of the sage fields, talking to him and Blue about my pack of dogs, seven in all. Daily, I walked my dogs through the sage. Daily, my father walked Blue along the flowering pathways. He wrote to me of wild parrots. I wrote to him of mischievous magpies. Our letters often crossed in the mail.

We wrote to each other of our delights—"flora and fauna reports," we called them. "I spotted a great blue heron," my father wrote with glee. I wrote back, "I have a barn owl that comes out at twilight." Peering off the bow of his boat, my father spotted an awkward manatee. I wrote him back of the small herd of buffalo a neighbor kept. Church bells pealed across Taos Valley. A tiny chapel graced the far end of my father's marina.

"What do you believe in, Dad?" I once asked my father, who clearly found God in nature. He chuckled in response.

"I believe in hedging my bets," he retorted, merriment dancing across his features.

From my father, I learned the value of humor and delight. My mother, Dorothy, was the love of his life. When she died an early death, my father sold the big house and bought his boat. He named the boat *Dorothy Two*, a sacrilegious homage to his late spouse. She would have appreciated his humor, and being remembered.

In the photo, my father wears a pale blue sweater, a

I love writing. I love the swirl and swing of words as they tangle with human emotions.

—JAMES MICHENER

gift from my mother before her passing. My little dog, Lily, a Westie, sometimes called a "white Scottie," sprawls watchful near my feet. Like Blue, she is a good companion. Like my father, I dote on my little dog. When I say, "Lily, you're a good dog," she thumps a bonny tail. From wherever my father and Blue are now, I sense they watch us with approval. I write of my joys, and theirs.

TASKS

1. Limiting Beliefs: Often, we make decisions based on beliefs that we take as truth—they are beliefs, after all—but just because we believe them does not make them true. Quickly fill in the following:

   Writers are . . .
   Writers are . . .
   Writers are . . .
   Writers are . . .
   Writers are . . .

   Look at your list. Are you holding negative beliefs about writers? Convert the negatives into positives. Can you find examples of writers who positively embody the qualities you have described?

2. Media Deprivation: For a whole week, deprive yourself of media as much as possible. When I offer this tool to my classes, I am always met with resistance—and explanations of how it is impossible to be a responsible adult without checking email. I understand this, and am not asking you to sabotage your job. However, I am asking you to eliminate as much media as you possibly can. How little time can you spend on your phone or in your email? Can you take a break from social media, TV, podcasts? This

is one of the most resisted—and most powerful—
tasks that I have created. Often those who resist it
the most are the ones who have the most profound
breakthroughs.

3. Treating Yourself like a Precious Object: While
you are engaging in media deprivation, this is the
perfect time to spend extra time pampering, spoiling, and being kind to yourself. You may find that
during media deprivation, you have a lot of extra
time. Can you indulge yourself this week? Perhaps
it is a hot bath, a massage, a nap? A break for hot
chocolate and people-watching? An extra Artist
Date? Please give yourself one treat, break, or adventure every day this week.

4. The Wall: At this point in the process, it is normal
to hit The Wall. Remember, it is digging under The
Wall rather than trying to scramble over it that gets
us across. When we hit The Wall, the trick is to be
willing to write badly—but to keep going. Recommit to your daily quota, your Morning Pages, Artist
Dates, and walks. I like to post a note on my desk:
"Great Creator, you take care of the quality, I'll take
care of the quantity."

5. Delight: In or out of your house, find an object that
delights you. It might be a photo of a beloved, a
tulip stand, a puppy pulling on its leash in the park.
Sit and write about that delight for five minutes.
What is delightful? How does it make you feel?
What does it evoke for you? Note your mood when
you are done writing. Has it lifted?

CHECK IN

1. How many days did you do your Morning Pages
this week? Are you able to get to them quickly and
do them without interruption or distraction?

2. Did you take your Artist Date? What was it? How was it? Did you experience synchronicity, optimism, or a sense of a benevolent higher power? All three?

3. Did you take your walks? Are you able to do them alone and without distraction? Did you try walking out with a question and seeing if you returned home with an answer?

4. Did you hit your daily quota? How many pages are you into your project? Do you feel a sense of excitement as you watch your page count building?

WEEK SIX

CELEBRATE YOUR ACHIEVEMENT

Hurrah! As you complete the six weeks, it is time to both celebrate what you have accomplished, and to plan for the future. You now have an extensive toolkit to support you as a productive and prolific writer. As you continue onward with your project, you will simultaneously be prepared for the next steps. Once you finish your first draft, you will be guided in how to polish, rewrite, and share it. It is my hope that you will look back to the essays in this handbook as you need them going forward, using this book as a support kit to write for life.

FIRST DRAFTS

Ahhh. You breathe a sigh of relief. Your first draft is done. How do you know it's done? You've written your story start to finish. Your ending may seem abrupt, but that's better than dragged out. Knowing when your draft is done calls for intuition. You "sense" your ending. You feel "written out." There is no magic formula telling you to stop. Instead, you *feel* that your draft is at an end.

I recently wrote a play without an ending in sight. "How does this play end?" I asked myself in vain. Scene after scene kept unfolding. I looked for clues for a proper ending, but each scene was a cliffhanger saying, "Not yet." I was reaching the proper length for a play. With no end in sight, audiences would grow bored. And then, one night of writing like any other, I got an ending. Called *True Love,* the play ended in a kiss. Too sentimental? No, for this play it was exactly right—the sudden, unexpected clinch marking the end.

I had written plays before, but always with at least a glimmering of an ending. This play taught me a valuable lesson: trust yourself. Trust your material. Trust that you will know. I was being asked to rely on instinct and intuition over intellect. Having learned that lesson, I teach it now. Trust yourself.

You've written your book, play, or movie, and you know it better than anyone else. You'll find your energy dropping away if you try to write past your natural ending. Instead, be prepared to be surprised. Allow your characters the last word. They will signal you, "Time to stop. We're finished."

It helps to think of your project in thirds. The first third introduces your characters, and their question or problem. The second third traces the question or problem through time. The third and final third answers the question or solves the problem.

Thought of this way, it is easy to know your ending. It is when the question is answered or the problem solved. If there is no resolution, keep writing. If there is a resolution, stop writing. The satisfaction of a draft occurs when we go, "Ah-ha." We have solved the problem or question. An unsatisfactory draft occurs when we leave the problem or question unanswered, or when the wrong answer is given.

Let us say we are writing a draft on love. The question is, "Will he or she find true love?" The wrong answer is, "He or she got the job." If your draft answers correctly, you will know it. There is an almost audible *ping* when the answer slots into view. There is an inner sense of completion that tells you, "Enough."

This may sound vague to you, but the feeling is anything but vague. If you try to stop your draft too soon or carry it on too late, your sixth sense will kick in. It

The pages are still blank, but there is a miraculous feeling of the words being there, written in invisible ink and clamoring to become visible.

—VLADIMIR NABOKOV

is an internal beeper which beeps "wrong." You do not need to worry. We all have this vital sixth sense. And so, I say again, trust yourself. Trust that the story you've told knows its ending. It will signal to you. Trust your draft.

SECOND DRAFTS

"Whew," we think when we finish the first draft of a project. We feel the flush of accomplishment, job well done. It is a triumphant moment. We may feel elated but spent. Now is the time to pause, to let our writing settle. A day, a week, a month—sooner or later, it will be time for more work, time for our second draft.

We begin the second-draft process not by writing, but by reading. We read the first draft through, encountering rough spots and smooth sailing. In parts, our first draft feels impossibly bad—in other parts, impossibly good. Overall, our manuscript is promising but flawed. Our job now is to fix it. And how do we do that?

To begin with, we check our attitude. Are we prepared to do more work? Or do we dig our heels in, saying our draft is good already? Make no mistake: writing involves rewriting. A first draft is exactly that: a first draft. Now it is time for a second draft, a draft of improvement. To begin with, we must surrender our ego's resistance to change. We must be open-minded enough to welcome change. But how do we know what it is? Here is how.

You've written a first draft and you've read it through. Now it's time to read it through again, this time, pen in hand. You are going to read, outlining as you read. For example, you will write:

Pages 1–4: introducing the main character
Pages 5–9: introducing "the problem"
Pages 10–15: a first attempt to solve the problem

Going through your draft, you will name—and claim—the people, places, and events that occur. Outlining tells you your structure. Sometimes you may see an immediate "fix." A character may appear early, and then disappear until far too late. If you spot this trouble, you will cure it by having the character appear again sooner. Sometimes a simple shuffling of the scenes' order is all that's required.

I use legal pads when I outline. I place page numbers to the left, and content of scenes to the right. I try to use one line per entry. I scroll through my entire draft. I jot down the significant information. It may take me an hour or two to complete my outline, but it is time well spent. Outlining brings clarity. A well-executed outline resembles a train track, with each entry a tie.

After you execute a full outline, make a copy of it. Your first outline tells you exactly what you have. Your second outline is for making changes. Tape the two outlines to the wall near your writing station. Now, dig in and go to work. What changes does your outline show you that you need? Are there scenes that need to be added? Where? Jot a note on your second outline. Are there scenes that should be cut? Cut them on your second outline. Moving down your "train track" of scenes, add and subtract as needed. You are making a blueprint of what you will need to write. Don't be surprised if whole scenes come to mind. Simply jot a note to yourself and keep moving on your track. Go all the way down your outline. No skipping ahead, no "real" writing. Your work with this task keeps you from getting lost in your rewrite.

You have a record of your first draft, and a blueprint for your second draft. Now you are ready to write. Starting at the top of your track, move an entry at a time, making the changes you have planned. Do the entries in order, although you may be tempted to skip ahead. Working in this orderly fashion, go from start to finish.

Writing is like driving a car at night in the fog. You can only see as far as your headlights, but you can make the whole trip that way.

—E. L. DOCTOROW

Congratulations! You have now executed a successful second draft. To move on from here, simply repeat the process you have learned. Read through your second draft, outline your second draft, copy your second draft outline. Moving from top to bottom of your track, note on the copied outline any further changes that you see. Is your story more clear? The objectivity of the outline leads to clarity. Clarity leads to success.

CHOOSING FRIENDS WISELY

"To thine own self be true, thou canst not be false to any man." What do we mean, "To thine own self be true"? We mean to listen to ourselves, most especially to our misgivings, those hunches, inklings, intuitions that tell us we are straying from our path. All of us have an inner compass that signals to us when we go astray, when we go along with an agenda that is not in our best interests.

The compass may express itself as a sinking feeling, butterflies in the stomach, a tightening of the chest, even shallowness of breath. These physical symptoms mirror our psychic discomfort. We intuitively sense what we do not perhaps put in words.

All of us have radar that scans our emotional terrain, signaling "safe" or "not safe." The radar is our gift of discernment. "Danger," it warns. Listening to our radar, we steer a safe course. Evaluating the situation we find ourselves in, our radar is indispensable. Evaluating people, it helps us choose our friends.

As writers, we are vulnerable. Our imaginations are well-honed. This means that we may concoct stories to soothe our psyches. When our radar sounds, we may invent a storyline to explain it. Rather than receive a warning, we may make up a tale that messes with our wishes. Yes, as writers we are gullible. We stretch our intellects to devise a narrative to our own liking.

My pen shall heal, not hurt.
—L. M. MONTGOMERY

Let us say a friend wants our support on a risky venture. Our radar—our inner compass—sounds an alarm: stay away. But we don't want to hurt our friend's feelings, and so we turn the knife of discernment on ourselves. We're paranoid, we tell ourselves. The venture only *seems* unstable. Against our better judgment, in the face of our radar, we decide to invest. Here we are at risk. We are practicing a tricky form of dishonesty: we are not being true to ourself. Acting a lie—our good faith—we are false not only to ourself but to our friend.

"To thine own self be true" requires self-honesty. We must attend to those fleeting "twinges" that warn us we are off track. As writers, we must be on the alert for trustworthy friends and readers, those people that our radar signals "all clear." Listening closely, listening to our "gut," we find friendships that are generous and supportive. Failing to attend to our radar, we find ourself saddled with relationships that are dangerous to our self-worth and our work.

It may sound dramatic, to find our work and our worth so closely bound together. But a writer is tied closely to his work. Let us say we have one more time ignored our radar, and placed our work in dangerous hands. A jealous reader can sabotage our self-esteem and impede our chances for success. Author Sonia Choquette showed her first draft to a jealous reader. "Is English your second language?" the reader sniped. Wounded by this feedback, Sonia buried her book and her dream of being a writer for ten long years. I pried the book loose from its hiding place and found it quite good. I became for Sonia a believing mirror. And with my encouragement, she brought the book to the light of day, and the attention of Random House, which successfully published it. Sonia's story has a happy ending: she's now written a dozen books. But she can never play catchup for the ten years of writing lost.

"To thine own self be true" demands of us that we

have character, that old-fashioned word. It takes character, and alert attention, to successfully gauge the character or lack of character of others. Consulting our radar, our inner compass, leads us carefully and well. As we face what we find, we are well served. We are seeking friends and readers with integrity, another old-fashioned word. We—and our work—deserve the dignity of well-chosen companions.

FEEDBACK

You've completed a second, perhaps even a third draft. You've taken your project as far as you can on your own. Now you are eager to show your work to readers and garner feedback. Feedback is the acid test. How well does your draft hold up? You want the opinions of others, but not just any others. You are looking now for believing mirrors, persons who are generous, who believe in you and your strength. Persons who are not jealous. Persons who understand your goal: excellence. Believing mirrors are rare and to be treasured.

Canvasing your friends for believing mirrors, you must yourself be hardheaded. Who among your potential readers is jealous? Not, perhaps, a problem in day-to-day exchanges, but a fatal flaw in a believing mirror. You are looking for those who are generous, and you want more than one. While you will weigh all feedback carefully, you do not want to give any single reader too much power. And so you select at least two readers, believing mirrors both.

You distribute your work to your believing mirrors, those people who wish you and your work well, and have no axe to grind. You tell them you'd like to hear their responses in two weeks' time. Then you settle in to wait. Two weeks is a short time, but be prepared to feel it is an eternity. To make the time pass quickly and productively, read your draft yourself. What do you think of it? Are there changes you'd like to make? Take notes detailing your impressions. Time allowing, read your draft a second time. Strive for objectivity as you jot down notes a second time.

I have a believing mirror in my friend of fifty-four years, Gerard Hackett. Levelheaded, even hardheaded, he can be depended upon to give me honest feedback. I recently showed him a draft of a new book I was working on.

"Good, but scrambled," came back his verdict. "The first hundred pages are fine. The second hundred pages need work. You're missing a cohesive structure."

I received Gerard's feedback with gratitude. He was not a writer, but rather a fine reader. His layman's notes pinpointed my writing's strengths and flaws. Thanks to Gerard, I had a sense of direction. I knew not to monkey with the first hundred pages. Rather, to focus on the book's second half, seeking not style, but structure.

It is fair game, when seeking feedback, to give a gentle guideline. "I'd like you to focus on the draft's strengths. Tell me what works, and why." It is my experience that focusing on strengths amplifies those strengths. Focusing on weaknesses amplifies those weaknesses—not what you want to do.

"What did you like?" and "What did you not like?" are two valid questions. Ask them *after* you have been told your project's strengths. "What would you like to see more of?" and "What would you like to see less of?" are two fruitful further questions.

Now you are ready to listen. One reader at a time, collect your feedback. Listen carefully to your believing mirrors. Take notes on their notes, and ask for clarification and amplification as needed. Overall, is your draft good? We hope yes. What changes, if any, does your reader recommend? Ask for an overview detailing specific strengths and weaknesses. Ask, was your draft enjoyable to read?

Listen to your reader's critique without defending yourself. Remember that you have invited their candid opinion. How do their notes compare with your own? Is there a consensus of necessary changes? Thank your reader for their time, trouble, and objectivity.

Now move on to your second reader. One more time, listen to your reader's review without defensiveness. Bear in mind that you have invited their analysis, however harsh it may appear. Once again, compare your notes with your reader's. Compare this reader's notes with the prior. Again, do you find a consensus? Remember, such feedback is invaluable. Ask point-blank if their reading experience was enjoyable. We hope, yes.

Remember that feedback that is vague or shaming is toxic feedback. If you receive some, cast it aside. Your choice of a believing mirror is at fault—not your draft.

Remember that your feedback will reflect the biases and expertise of your believing mirror. Try to take this into account. You may have inadvertently hit on a sore spot. Discredit any feedback that feels unduly heated. You are after coolheaded objectivity. Comparing several reader's reports may yield you a consensus—or one report may resonate as more accurate than the others. When it does, you will sense an inner "ah-ha" as the feedback points you in a direction that resonates with your intentions for the draft.

Remember, feedback is intended to be useful. Constructive feedback strengthens your project. Feedback that is overly complimentary is useless. You are after feedback that is levelheaded, accurately reflecting and responding to your draft with its foibles, follies, and flaws. A believing mirror gives you both positive feedback and accuracy.

Remember that goodwill is invaluable. Remind yourself of the good intentions of your believing mirrors. Be grateful for their fair-minded feedback. Weigh their opinions against your own. Balance the feedback of others with your personal judgments. Remember that feedback is a prescription: we want to be "fed" back.

Continue to garner feedback from your readers. Remember, always, that their feedback serves a constructive purpose: to make your work better. You are served here by containment, showing your work to only a select few, and only after you yourself are satisfied with the draft. Showing your work to too many, and too soon, invites trouble. Remember, the first rule of magic is containment. Showing your work too early asks for difficulty. Protect your work by using discretion. Show it once it is ready to be seen. Receive your feedback gladly. Thank your readers for their help. You are ready now to move on to a polish.

POLISHING YOUR DRAFT

"Does it say what I mean? Does it mean what I say?" These are ultimate questions we must ask our polish draft. Polish comes from clarity, and clarity often comes from simplicity. Put simply, we are striving to communicate. And that communication must hold first place in our minds. The rest is just window dressing.

"What am I trying to say," we must ask ourselves. The answer should be both bold and brief. Reading it over, we must think, "Yes! That's it." Sometimes what we are trying to say and what we've said are two differing things. In such cases, we must choose: Which is it to be? We need to throw our hat in the ring. Either we must alter what we've said, or we must emphasize the saying of it.

This winter past, I wrote my play *True Love,* featuring two couples well-suited to each other. I called the play

I write entirely to find out what I'm thinking.

—JOAN DIDION

True Love because that was its theme—the resiliency and generosity of love. I showed the play to a director who wanted to know, "Where's the conflict? Where's the bitterness?" I heard his questions with dismay.

"There is no conflict. They're beyond bitterness," I told him. Then I went back to the play and underscored "true love." I ended the play with a kiss. Polishing the play, I saw it needed more tenderness. After all, what is true love, if not tender?

When you polish a piece of work, you make minor changes indicated by your readers and yourself. Now is not the time for major revisions. By now, your draft is what it is. You are simply going to make it more so. You may tweak a scene or two to emphasize your theme, but your theme is by now apparent. You will be checking now for clarity.

There are two further questions to ask yourself: Does it begin where it should, and end where it should? Very often, the answers to these questions are "It should begin later, and it should end sooner." Bear in mind that you are trimming away unnecessary fat, aiming for a lean, readable draft. "Do I repeat myself?" you might profitably ask. If so, cut the offending scene. Overdoing your theme is as offensive as not making it clear enough. Your future readers can be trusted. If your writing is overall clear, they will get what you are driving at. Satisfied that you have answered all the questions satisfactorily, you now have in hand a polished draft.

RESISTING TOXIC CRITICISM

I opened my mailbox this morning and found inside a note from a fellow writer.

"Ouch!" the note exclaimed. "Is my book as bad as this review?" A clipping was enclosed. Its tone was hostile, damningly condescending, yet vague. The writer was understandably wounded. I placed a call to tell him that I had enjoyed his book, and that the reviewer was an idiot. I was angry on his behalf.

When a critical arrow is accurate, our writer's response is, "Ah-ha! Now I get it!" All writers, no matter how good they are, yearn to be better, and criticism which helps us toward this aim is received gladly. The criticism which harms a writer is inaccurate, often vague, and shaming. This criticism causes pain and is not on the mark. It is received by the writer not with "Ah-ha!" but with "Arghhh!" We yearn to be better, but toxic criticism weakens, rather than strengthens, our craft.

I am thinking now of my friend Ted. He wrote a marvelous mystery which he showed to the wrong person.

As a first-time novelist, Ted labored long and hard over his manuscript, and then he paid one hundred dollars to have it read and critiqued by a literary agent. The criticism he received back was toxic criticism. The agent wrote, "This book is half good and half bad. I can't really tell you how to fix it. Perhaps the most useful thing I could say is try another." Ted received this criticism bravely and took it to heart. He briefly set about trying to write another, but the damning criticism had wounded his writer. He was afraid to trust his instincts about what was good and what was bad.

Ted put the book in a bottom drawer. It was eight years later that I coaxed him into showing me the draft. It was wonderful, and I told Ted that. But the damage was too severe, and he did not believe me. After all, I was his friend.

"Doesn't it need a wholesale rewrite?" he asked. "I'm afraid the book is bad in ways I can't see."

"No," I told him. "I think it's ready to go. Let's send it to another agent." Ted reluctantly surrendered his book, but his opinion of the book as deeply flawed lingered. When the agent told him the book was ready for

Everybody is talented because everybody who is human has something to express.

—BRENDA UELAND

submission, he second-guessed the agent. Rather than give permission for a go-ahead, he told her, "I think it needs a lot of work." The agent was astonished and annoyed by Ted's attitude. She withdrew her offer to represent the book, and Ted took her rejection as the proof he needed that his book was bad.

In my years as a writer, I have found stories like Ted's to be all too common. I am often asked, "Julia, with your work on creative unblocking, aren't you afraid you're unblocking a lot of bad writing?" Thinking of Ted, I reply, "No. A lot of very good work is blocked."

As a rule of thumb, we must be very careful about the criticism we receive. First off, we must always show our work to believing mirrors, those people who wish us well and enjoy reading for the sake of reading. Ideally, more than one reader must be sought out, and all are constructive. But it is possible that we will run into toxic criticism, and we must be alert for the earmarks of it. Is it vague, shaming, or damning? We must allow for the possibility that a toxic critic may simply be jealous of our work.

My crime novel *The Dark Room* received promising early reviews. The book was good, and I was justifiably proud of it. Then came a damning review. The critic wondered what a "new-age guru" was doing writing in such a different genre. He discovered that the hero loved Carl Jung, whom he clearly did not. A Freudian, his review attacked Jung at great length. My book was barely mentioned, damned by association. I found myself stung by the unfair criticism. I felt I should don sackcloth and ashes. Instead, I resorted to a favorite trick. I used humor to disarm the sting. I wrote,

> *This little poem goes out to Bill Kent*
> *He must feel awful the way that he spent*
> *His time critiquing Carl Jung*
> *Instead of on the book I'd done.*

Humor is the very best antidote for toxic criticism. I told my friend Ted that he should try a dose of it to get over his wounding. Ted wrote,

I asked a man to criticize
But just received a pack of lies
The book was bad, my critic said
Is it a wonder I wish him dead?

Ted and I chuckled over his skewering of the malevolent agent. He resolved to be more discerning and tough-minded about the criticism he took to heart. A few days later, I received a call from Ted.

"I'm writing again," he told me. I was thrilled to hear it. "I can't believe how much I've missed it." Ted sounded jubilant, happier than in years.

"Writing is healing," I told him. "Keep going."

HOW DO YOU KNOW WHEN IT'S FINISHED?

It's twilight. The mountains loom lilac as a long day draws to a close. Tonight is a full moon, blessing what I write. But I may not write at all. My project is drawing to a close. Finished. It is intuition which brings me a sense of closure. I have written "enough." Putting pen to page, I scan my emotional horizon, searching for a last topic. But my search yields nothing. I am indeed finished.

Being done with a piece of work is a feeling based on facts. I have written what I planned to write, and perhaps then some. I've drawn heavily on my inner well, taking care to replenish it with Artist Dates. But now, reaching within for further words, I find none. No words? No words. But instead of panic, I feel calm. I've written words enough.

How do I know? When a project is finished, there is

calm, a steady sense of satisfaction. There is no urgency to go further. Done is done. Our writer is satisfied. Scanning for further work, no topic looms. Instead, there is a feeling of completion. I say "feeling" knowing that sounds vague. But the feeling is not vague. It is distinctive. It feels different, more peaceful, than times during the writing when I have felt stalled. This is not stalled. This is finished, done, completed. You may feel a little hollow. Suddenly there is space, where before, your draft was a constant companion. Do not be surprised if you feel at loose ends. You *are* at loose ends. For comfort, you may take to the page, writing out your feelings.

"Well, I think I'm done," you might write. "I have nothing further to add. I feel oddly empty. No, I feel amputated, as if a limb has been lopped off. That sounds dramatic, but it *is* dramatic, finishing a piece of work. I wonder what I'll do next."

Wondering "what next" is a symptom of your writer's identity. Already, you miss writing, which tells you that your ending is really a beginning. You love to write.

The silver moon climbs the sky. It is a harvest moon, and what I am harvesting is my project. Moonlight drifts through my window. It is serene and steady. If I let myself feel it, I, too, am serene and steady. "Job well done," I tell myself. I *love* to write.

There is no real ending. It's just the place where you stop the story.

—FRANK HERBERT

TASKS

1. Recommit to Your Process: You have completed the six weeks, and your draft should be well underway. It is now time to recommit to your tools. Are you doing your Morning Pages every day? Are you doing your Artist Dates and walks? Is it time to increase your dates or your walks? Are you meeting your daily quota?

2. Containment: Draw a circle. Inside the circle, write the names of those people in your life who are safe for your writer. These are people who are encouraging, generous, thoughtful, and have your best interests at heart. Now, outside the circle, write the names of the people in your life who are not safe for your writer. They may be blocked themselves, overly critical, mean-spirited, or judgmental. Protect your writer from these people. Do not share your early drafts or in-process thoughts with them. Practice self-love by practicing containment around those people in your life who are toxic to your writer.

3. Choosing Friends Wisely: Looking back at your circle, choose a few friends from inside your circle who might be the people you will share your draft with when you are ready. Perhaps you would like to reach out to them and ask if they would be willing to read your draft when it is done.

4. Celebrate Your Achievement: Congratulations! It is time to celebrate all you have accomplished over the past six weeks. Can you plan an all-day Artist Date? Can you buy yourself a special treat or give yourself an extra break? Please spoil yourself!

5. Plan for the Future: As you move forward with your draft, hitting your daily quota and taking care of your writer with the tools you have well established, you can plan for the future. This week addresses how to tell when your draft is done, and how to move into second drafts, polishing, and receiving feedback from safe friends. It is my hope that going forward you will use this book as a handbook, looking back at essays as you need them and remembering that you are not alone as you write for life.

CHECK IN

1. How many days did you do your Morning Pages this week? Are you able to get to them quickly and do them without interruption or distraction?

2. Did you take your Artist Date? What was it? How was it? Did you experience synchronicity, optimism, or a sense of a benevolent higher power? All three?

3. Did you take your walks? Are you able to do them alone and without distraction? Did you try walking out with a question and seeing if you returned home with an answer?

4. Did you hit your daily quota? How many pages are you into your project? Do you feel a sense of excitement as you watch your page count building?

INDEX

ABOUT THE AUTHOR

Robert Stivers

Hailed by *The New York Times* as "The Queen of Change," **JULIA CAMERON** is credited with starting a movement in 1992 that has brought creativity into the mainstream conversation—in the arts, in business, and in everyday life. She is the bestselling author of more than forty books, fiction and nonfiction; a poet, songwriter, filmmaker, and playwright. Commonly referred to as "The Godmother" or "High Priestess" of creativity, her tools are based in practice, not theory, and she considers herself "the floor sample of her own toolkit." *The Artist's Way* has been translated into forty languages and sold over five million copies to date.